Conten

D1536454

Disclaimer

Testimonials

"Today we are in an ethics deficit. It's not pretty and it makes the job of the communicator even more challenging. We all have to be experts. Mark McClennan's Ethical Voices *will help you become that expert. Through 100 real-world ethics incidents with advice from global industry leaders, you will be on the path to being the ethics steward for your organization."*—**Gini Dietrich, founder and CEO, Spin Sucks**

"At a time of great social, political and economic turbulence, and complexity, more than ever, public relations and communications professionals are being called upon by their organizations' leadership for their advice and counsel on critical issues, important decisions, and ethical behavior. As a leading voice on ethics and integrity in public relations, in this essential book, McClennan lays out a straightforward, clear-cut framework—with practical examples— to help guide professionals as they are called upon to help lead amidst today's uncertainty and turmoil."—**Ray Kotcher, Former CEO and Chairman, Ketchum**

Acknowledgments

This book is only possible because so many people selflessly and honestly shared their experience, insights, challenges, and failures. I appreciate every single one of you giving so much.

I owe special thanks to my wife, Maggie, and my two boys, Joseph and Jack, who understood when Daddy needed quiet for interviews and holed up working on this book.

Thanks to Judy DeRango Wicks, APR, Fellow PRSA, and Kirk Hazlett, APR, Fellow PRSA, for being my first readers and for your friendship and guidance over the decades.

I want to thank PRSA for graciously allowing me to use their Code of Ethics to create a foundation for the book. It has been my ethical guidepost my entire career and has helped countless others understand the importance of advocacy, honesty, expertise, independence, loyalty, fairness, free flow of information, competition, disclosure of information, safeguarding confidences, conflicts of interest, and enhancing the profession.

Finally, thanks to Maria Russell, APR, Fellow PRSA, for first opening my eyes to the possibilities and ethical responsibilities of public relations, and Dave Close for being a great mentor.

CHAPTER 1

Introduction

When most people think of ethics, they think of Socrates, Aristotle, Plato, or Confucius. If they ever attended an ethics course, they think about deontology, teleology, virtue, patriarchal, and feminist ethical theories. They think about big scandals—from Enron to BP to Volkswagen. Unfortunately, most people think ethics is dry, boring, something they learned in school, or something they are required to attend once a year to meet human resources requirements.

They couldn't be more wrong.

Ethics is at the center of human development, human failure, and human triumph throughout society for the past 4,000 years. It is the crux of the soap opera of human history. It is what is behind jealousy, envy, betrayal, murder, and so many other human failings.

Luckily, most communication professionals won't have to deal with backstabbing murder or a scandal the size of Volkswagen or Enron. Most won't have to take the steps Paula Pedene took to expose the scandal at the Veterans' Administration. But there are thousands of ethical pitfalls and innocuous requests that can lead to significant trouble down the road, if you watch out every day of your career.

As the host of *Ethical Voices*, a podcast on public relations ethics, I have interviewed leading public relations executives about how they have handled ethical challenges. Since 2018, I have conducted in-depth interviews with more than 150 executives, asking them three core questions:

- What is the most significant ethics challenge you have faced in your career?
- What do you see as the most significant ethics challenges facing the profession?
- What was the best ethics-related advice you ever received?

These interviews sparked some amazing discussions. If you listen to all the interviews, it is more than 500,000 words on ethics and 70 hours of fascinating conversations. This book distills what was learned to provide practical advice, guidance, and examples to public relations professionals facing their own ethical challenges.

The challenge I faced as I was writing this book was to think about how to organize this overwhelming wealth of ethical advice, experience, and insight. After much reflection, I realized we already had a great guide for ethical thinking. A guide that has served public relations professionals for more than 70 years—The Public Relations Society of America's (PRSA's) Code of Ethics. The Code and PRSA have been there throughout my career and ethics training. Joining PRSA was the single greatest thing I did to help my career.

I approached PRSA, and they agreed to let me use it as a framework for this book. While the framework follows PRSA's Code of Ethics six professional values and six provisions of conduct, the categorizations are all mine and do not reflect the views or official content from PRSA.

In some cases, interviews could fit under multiple topics, and I simply chose the one I liked best. In some cases, I extended the values and provisions beyond the guidance PRSA offers.

Hopefully, these voices, stories, and advice will be a reference and a guide for professionals for some of the many ethical challenges they may face in their careers. They can learn from the advice, wisdom, and horrible mistakes of others, so they can see issues in advance, and be better prepared.

The interviews in this book are not transcribed verbatim. Some light editing was done for brevity and clarity, but other than that, I am letting the voices speak in their own words and tone.

Dive in, listen to the voices, and start your journey in training your ethical mind.

CHAPTER 2

Advocacy

When most people think of public relations (PR) professionals, they immediately think of advocacy. It is drummed into the heads of thousands of PR students every year—public relations professionals are responsible advocates for those we represent. We work to advance our organizations and shape public opinion.

But there are limits to how far we should go. Public relations professionals are trained in how to create campaigns that sway behavior and opinion. We have superpowers that can change the country, and the world. To paraphrase Uncle Ben and Aunt May from *Marvel's Spiderman*—with this superpower, comes great responsibility.

The PRSA Code of Ethics makes this abundantly clear. Advocacy is the first value in the code.

> *Advocacy:* We serve the public interest by acting as responsible advocates for those we represent. We provide a voice in the marketplace of ideas, facts, and viewpoints to aid informed public debate.

But what is responsible, ethical advocacy? What happens when you know getting your point across is essential to saving your job, saving your company, or saving the planet? What happens when your boss wants to advocate unethically? Following is advice on how to handle these and other issues.

Should We Advocate?

Before we look at advocacy, we need to look at two questions everyone should ask themselves before they begin. Should we do it in the first place, and on what topics should we engage?

There are so many pressing issues on which companies can take a stand. Is immigration more important than curing cancer or protecting the environment? You can't engage everywhere. If you do, your resources will be spread thin, and at best, you will be a pebble thrown into the ocean. At the worst, your employees will think your management team is like a soccer team of seven-year-olds—chasing after each new shiny object and not being committed to anything.

There are two different points of view on the subject. **David Herrick,** the managing principal of EthicOne, has conducted extensive research and found:

> A little over half of the companies we looked at engage in issues that are outside of their day-to-day business and product offerings but are related. A health care company could work to help low-income people afford health insurance or get more sidewalks built so that people can exercise. The other not quite half of the companies we studied were not doing those things yet, but they were all actively engaged discussions about it. They are asking:
>
> How should we engage with our communities?
>
> This is a major focus in boardrooms across the country, and is another area where communications leaders need to be part of those conversations.
>
> We all must ask:
>
> 1. Where do we engage on an issue?
> 2. How do we engage?
> 3. Is it true to our core?
> 4. Is it true to our values?
>
> If so, let's do it. If not, maybe this is someone else's issue to carry. But that decision-making process must be had, because consumers, and especially younger ones, will not excuse corporate absenteeism. If you're absent on issues customers expect you to be involved with, you may get punished in the marketplace.

Dr. Holly Overton, associate professor at the University of South Carolina and a senior research fellow with the Arthur W. Page Center for Integrity in Public Communication, takes this a step further when it comes to *hot button* issues.

We're facing a number of societal issues that have truly divided our nation—climate change, health care reform, gun violence, racial injustice, and issues related to gender and marriage equality.

Public expectations of companies have evolved over the past few decades. Fifty years ago, it was widely accepted that companies existed to increase profits. As we entered the 21st century, the public increasingly developed the expectation that companies will contribute to society in some way, shape, or form.

This is where the whole notion of the *triple bottom line* became commonplace—profit, people, and planet.

Today, societal expectations are shifting again, and the public is increasingly turning to companies to be advocates for social change and to solve society's issues. We're seeing more and more companies engage in risk by taking public stances on sociopolitical issues that transcend organizational interests and are aimed at the betterment of society. However, companies are understandably nervous about stance-taking and are still seeking guidance on when and how to speak out, and when not to.

Think about Nike and the Colin Kaepernick campaign. That sparked a lot of controversy. And as a scholar, this example was particularly interesting to me, and I did a number of studies about the Kaepernick ad. Some other examples include Gillette and the #MeToo campaign, and Dick's Sporting Goods and gun control. PR professionals are still trying to navigate how to balance public demands for action with their organizational values. They're being put on the spot to prioritize ethics.

Some people think that having companies engage in controversial sociopolitical issues is very necessary, but there are others who feel that it's not the place for companies to enter the conversation. Much of that is underscored by the idea that companies are profit-seeking entities, and that their words and even sometimes their actions are considered to be insincere. There are also others who are somewhere in-between, arguing that the run-of-the-mill statement means nothing.

This challenge goes back to one of the Page Principles from the Arthur W. Page Society (Page 2022) that says, "Prove it with action. Public perception of an enterprise is determined 90% by what it does and 10% by what it says."

Not everyone agrees businesses should engage in advocacy, and communicators need to understand there are valid differences of opinion. **Rebekah Iliff**, founder of WriteVest, explains:

Don't let the wind shift you. You have to have a very strong sense of yourself particularly now, because there is all this noise and there are all these messages flying around. If you're a stakeholder or a shareholder, you're like, "Can you please just stay in your zone?" Ethics don't mean becoming a political activist when that's not your core business. Today it is being conflated. People think, "I have to 'show' my ethics." And the only way to show your ethics a lot of times when you're a company is to hook into whatever the "popular" topic of the day is.

I've had clients say, "We need to write a paper about political activism," because they think that that's going to make them relevant. I tell them no, because it doesn't have anything to do with your business.

No one is going to stop buying your widget if you don't say anything about some big headline that everyone's talking about. You don't just hook into something and become part of a conversation because you want to be relevant for five minutes. You've got to ask is that core to the business strategy? Is it going to set the company up for future success? Does it impact my shareholders?

When Delta's CEO came out and made a public statement about a social issue, the stock tanked overnight. The second it went back up enough to where I didn't lose money, I sold it all because this person, he should be flying airplanes and giving the best customer service.

The communications person advising him should be fired because they were only thinking, how are we going to get into a conversation? How are we going to get a press hit? Instead of asking what's going to happen to all of these hundreds of thousands of people that have bought into the Delta ethos, our paying customers, our shareholders?

That made all of them lose. Communicators have a responsibility to look at the business as a whole and to be able to push back on the C-suite.

Dr. Holly Overton provides some additional guidance for professionals struggling with the question of when to advocate.

There are still a lot of unknowns. People are still negotiating what corporate social responsibility means.

Companies are trying to respond, but at the same time, we're seeing a lot of examples where reputations are actually damaged by certain efforts that aren't embedded in core values, aren't responsibly and ethically communicated. People perceive that it's not a sincere effort. Motives matter. And the public sees that and is starting to hold companies accountable.

Corporate social advocacy is strategic risk. If you look at Nike and Colin Kapernik, they polarized some folks and lost some customers, but they gained even more. Ben & Jerry's has seen the same thing. It's embedded in the idea that they have a responsibility to stand up and speak up, and they have to do it explicitly.

There is no cookie-cutter approach. Turn to the research. Survey your audience, your job seekers, your current employees, your stakeholders. We're seeing a lot of studies that are finding just how much this matters to consumers. More people are saying, "This is a priority for me as a consumer. I will go to a different company and support that brand if they're being socially responsible."

Ethical Advocacy Advice

Beyond deciding when and where to engage in advocacy, communicators want to make sure their side prevails. It is human nature. But that can cause people to take things too far according to **Peter Loge**, associate professor of media and public affairs and director of the Project on Ethics and Political Communication at George Washington University. His advice transcends political communications:

> In politics everybody's right and righteous. Everybody wakes up in the morning thinking they're on the side of the angels. So, it's okay to lie a little bit, because the stakes are so high.
>
> They say, "sure this isn't quite true, but we'll fix it once we get elected." They say, "So much is at stake in this election. It's okay to cheat a little bit, because of the longer-term gain. The glorious magical ends that we can only see, justify whatever little, tiny nefarious needs we may have to tweak along the way." That's incredibly dangerous.
>
> A specific example of this was in the Alabama special Senate race several years ago. You had a Republican candidate who a lot of people thought was pretty awful. He was banned from local malls. A bunch of Democratic operatives looked at what Russian operatives were doing in the 2016 election and copied those tactics. They set up fake Facebook accounts, they spread online rumors. They pushed things that weren't true online. Their justification was, well, the stakes were so high. It's easy to say, "This moment's unique." The problem is, you're always then one election away from governing.
>
> We have to be careful that in doing the right thing, we don't become the bad guys.

Neil Foote, CEO of Foote Communications and president of the National Black Public Relations Society, believes in the power of unembellished truth to drive ethical action.

> The ongoing joke about PR folks is you make stuff up and put your spin on it. As a young reporter, I was probably one of those folks who were like, "Oh my gosh, PR, get out of here." Now that I've been doing it for almost 20 years, I realized that so much of what we do is so important about building the credibility and brand of our clients. What's particularly challenging for us as public relations professionals is making sure that we not only find

the best possible news angle and hooks for our clients, but that we don't fall in the trap what some of our clients want us to spin it so that the core facts and elements don't reflect the truth.

We must be as fact-based as possible. Stick to the facts, tell a good story. That's what's going to generate coverage nowadays. I advise many of my clients that we have to be extremely patient because unless you're willing to use some extreme angle with your story idea, no matter what it is, even if it's a book that doesn't have anything to do with politics or social justice or health or medical issues, we will have to navigate our way through the storm of noise. Navigation requires careful, conscious, hard work, and a good strategy that's born in facts, and is ethically sound.

Sherry Feldberg, principal, Leadership Journey, shares advice on what to do if your boss pressures you to act unethically:

Approach it calmly. Don't say "I can't believe you'd ask me to do this." Don't be highly emotional. Stay calm and make it clear that you'd like to have a conversation. Start by asking to have an open dialogue so that you can better understand their point of view. Don't be accusatory when you speak with them or use a lot of the "you, you, you." Then ask for the opportunity to express your thoughts and see if you can see each other's points of view and if that changes anything.

Most of the time that has worked well. It's a good approach. It's when people either are too afraid to say something, so they don't say anything, or they use a lot of emotion, that it goes south quickly.

Garland Stansell, APR, chief communications officer for Children's of Alabama, and 2019 National Chair of PRSA highlights another issue with advocacy and ethics—*the tyranny of urgency*:

There are more challenges from the compressed news cycle and the tyranny of urgency to be first. We used to have a long news cycle, then it went to a 24-h news cycle and now we may have 24 minutes or 24 seconds.

Because of technology, social media and changes in traditional media, there is more demand to be faster, quicker, and the first. Sometimes we don't make our best decisions when we're trying to be fast, quick, first, and it may create some ethical issues. Are we making sure that we have verified all of the facts and the information so that we are speaking from a place of trust, fact, and truthfulness? As communicators, we need to make sure that we are being as responsive as we can be, but are also taking the time to be thoughtful and deliberate, truthful, and factual in our responses.

Advocacy Ethics Issues in Action

When it comes to advocacy, companies are often attacked by those with opposing agendas. **Jim Hoggan,** founder, DeSmog blog, recommends "Don't confuse doing the right thing with being seen doing the right thing."

We always paid attention to the ethics of things. We didn't want to be caught on the wrong side of issues because, even if we didn't care about the issues and being ethical, it's bad for business to be smeared all over the front page of the paper.

One day I was hired to do crisis management for this big food company. They had a hepatitis A outbreak, and their sales dropped 80 percent. When they were interviewing me over a conference call to see whether they would hire me, this woman asked, "How would you approach this?"

I said, "Do the right thing. Be seen to be doing the right thing and don't get those two mixed up. Ultimately crisis management is a character test, and you need to think about it that way every day and every hour as you go through each of the tough decisions that you're making."

Angela Sinickas, CEO of Sinickas Communications, shares how she dealt ethically with people with an agenda.

I simply presented the indisputable facts on what had happened because there were tape recordings and transcripts. Address the issue head on. We had to do something like that with 20/20. They were going to do something on one of our clients but what they were saying was incorrect. By sharing the facts, they ended up having to find another security company to dump on. You can deal with agendas if they give you a chance to talk before they have their story written.

Advocacy pressure can also come from inside your organization. **Kim Sample,** president of the PR Council, provides guidance on how to deal with controversial clients and employee activism.

Every company has a right to PR counsel if they're going to listen and take action. But it's challenging right now because employees don't want to work for many businesses. I'll give a very specific example.

At two different times in my career, I did gratifying, important work for Ringling Brothers. Once helping them with their animal care program. I had another chance to work with them when I was at Emanate, but my employee base was not excited about the opportunity.

They could not support it because of the animal issues. We had to decline. You've got to understand what your employees care about, what they can feel good about working on, and make good choices.

Letting employees opt out is not enough in this age of employee activism. We need to help our employees understand that we are for-profit businesses, and we try to make great decisions, but they're not always going to be 100 percent in agreement with our decisions. Here are our values that we are operating in compliance with. Make sure to take time to talk people through things and answer questions in transparent, forthcoming ways.

Some industries present interesting advocacy challenges. **Loring Barnes,** APR, Fellow PRSA, has been active in the cannabis industry:

I've been on every side of it. I've not only been on the governmental and policy setting side as the Chair of my town's Selectboard, but I've also been counsel (unrelated to that) to a very interesting technology-driven organization in the cannabis sector. My job was to understand all sides. I read blogs and books on the topic that covered both ends of the spectrum. It studied the economic indicators that have been a driving force for the acceptance of cannabis and the unfolding medical and clinical research that indicates how cannabis product elements are changing the face of pharma and wellness.

Only by understanding all sides, could I stand before my town as a government leader and say, "I hear you. I have listened and I've gone out to do research." By doing that, I had upheld an ethical responsibility to understand all the concerns. Only by educating myself could I navigate them and advocate in a balanced way.

That's what ethics comes down to. It's approaching every issue and challenge from the middle and looking out at all the potential stakeholders. Creating a safe place where people can come and express their views, no matter how extreme, no matter how ill or under informed. I don't know that you ever satisfy everybody on a controversial issue. But what you can definitely agree with is that the process of having this conversation in an open forum where every citizen's voice was protected and matters.

Robin Schell, APR, fellow PRSA, senior counsel and partner at Jackson, Jackson & Wagner, distills the issue to a question every PR professional should ask themselves when they are engaging in advocacy.

"If you feel like it's taking a more manipulative turn, ask yourself, am I still on board?"

Five Key Takeaways

How do we practice ethical advocacy?

1. Always disclose for whom you work.
2. Escape the echo chamber and look at all sides.
3. Actions always speak louder than words.
4. Wanting something to be true doesn't make it true. Use data to back up your points.
5. It's a marathon, not a sprint. Successful advocacy takes time. Charge rarely happens by yourself.

CHAPTER 3

Honesty

Honesty is the best policy, yet all of us lie at some point or another in our lives. If you spend any time reading Kant, you realize that telling 100 percent of the truth 100 percent of the time is challenging. Do you tell the truth if someone wants to hurt someone you love and asks you where they are? Do you tell the truth when your significant other asks how they look in an outfit? Yet, that creates a dangerous slippery slope when people think it is okay to lie *sometimes*.

PRSA's Code of Ethics states:

> *Honesty*: We adhere to the highest standards of accuracy and truth in advancing the interests of those we represent and in communicating with the public.

What Is Truth?

There are entire philosophy books written on this topic. It requires some examination of conscience. Before we delve into honesty best practices in communication, it is important to ask what is truth?

Most people say truth is that which is in accordance with facts or reality. But sometimes, there are honest disputes where both people are telling the truth as they know it. When I'm talking to young professionals, I bring up the example of the gold and white or blue and black dress. You get passionate arguments on both sides, and both people are saying the truth based on their perception.

Jeff Hahn, the author of *Breaking Bad News*,[1] believes truth is a negotiated reality. He says:

> I've come to appreciate over all these years of doing crisis work the extent to which two sides of a story can both be true. It depends on perspective. The perspective of the stakeholders from all sides must be accounted for in order for there to be an authentic and ethical message that appears in the dialogue between the stakeholders.
>
> One of the more intriguing and psychologically challenging aspects of the craft is that as time moves forward, the truth in a particular moment may not stay the truth as things evolve. Truth is a negotiated reality, and one that is not stuck in time. It continues to be negotiated and replayed and reconstituted. We do that to ourselves. We reframe history all the time.

Robert Johnson, the former Head of TSA Communications and Host of PR Nation podcast, considers honesty to be one of the biggest ethical challenges facing PR pros today:

> The line is blurred today. People stretch, bend, blindfold the truth, they submit statements as the truth, when it's just opinion. Opinion has taken over.
>
> I'm old enough to remember the days when the opinions in the media were limited to certain parts of the broadcast or two pages of the newspaper. Now, it's across the spectrum. Our biggest ethical challenge is making sure that we are attuned to the truth, that we know how to wash all the opinion out of it, and that we don't necessarily accept that any media outlet is free from that problem.
>
> I see this in every media outlet. The celebrity journalist has taken over, everybody needs to get clicks and likes and views and shares on their social media channels. They have a tote board in the *Washington Post* newsroom where reporters can see how their stories are playing during the day with audiences. How does that benefit journalism?

---

[1] J. Hahn. 2020. *Breaking Bad News: 12 Essential Crisis Communication Tools*, Sky Harbor Farm Publishing.

It shouldn't be good enough for people to just assign a truth-telling label to someone who screams the loudest. But today if you talk enough about something and you say it like you mean it, the media, more often than not, is going to take that. If they agree with you, they will adopt it as the truth, if they don't, then they beat you over the head with it. You have to make sure that everything you say can be backed up and referenced.

José Manuel Velasco, past President of the Global Alliance for Public Relations and Communication Management, provides advice on PR's most important job—taking care of the truth:

The narrative must be very solid and be grounded in facts in context. It's important to put together the main message, and the context to give people the opportunity to understand the whole picture. The context is a very important part of the truth because it helps to understand why, under what circumstances, and for what things happen.

Sometimes, we are dealing with the perceptions more than facts. Stakeholders should have the opportunity to ask the organization why they made a decision. That's why, it's essential that the organization creates a system of emphatic listening. It's not about telling the stakeholders what they want to hear, but what is useful and true so that they can make their decision in relationship with the company.

You must organize conversations with all stakeholders. You must create safe spaces to host that dialogue, because sometimes we create channels to speak with the stakeholders only from our perspective. It's very important to show the stakeholders that you are taking consideration of their issues.

We must also be aware that as PR managers, we are serving our organization, but at the same time, we are serving the social trust. We have a social responsibility that goes beyond our companies.

Sometimes that could put us in an uncomfortable situation because they are paying our salaries, but at the same time, we are serving the public interest.

Truth is made up of facts and also emotions. Emotions are very important in our lives. To feel fear because you are fighting with a different or dangerous situation is a fact and an emotion. We must not separate facts from emotions.

Brands want to highlight their ethical actions, but that can lead to ethics-washing.

David Herrick, Managing Principal of EthicOne, counsels against it:

A company we've worked closely with found through market research that if they talk about ethics and values with no proof points, they harm themselves with their customers who actually trust them less.

When they backed it up with true data points and true facts about how they operated, how they behave, how they received honors and designations when it came to their ethical business conduct, then it became a powerful incentive for customers and employees.

The first step is not to go talk about how ethical you are. The first step is to get your policies, procedures, practices in place so you can actually deliver on ethics and trust.

Honesty Ethics Issues in Action

Dave Close, retired Managing Director of MSL Boston, put it into perspective when he discusses how little *fails* with honesty can lead to unethical requests:

We're set up from movies and TV that the bad guy is really bad, and he's going to be a scowling guy with evil intent who is going to instruct people to lie and do terrible things. That does not reflect reality. What happens is almost every day in business there are a lot of little ethical decisions that you must make. Almost all of them, at least at the start, are not that big of deal. It's a little thing, it's trim here and there. But if you go along with it, you can set yourself down a path where the situation becomes more dire.

I worked with a lot of startup companies that had very hard-charging people, and they would move very quickly, and some-times, it would be kind of sloppy. Many of these companies did IPOs and were then subject to SEC oversight.

One client wanted us to write and issue a press release declaring a big sale. I hadn't heard of this big sale. I started poking around and asking questions. It turned out that it was just a letter of intent.

As a small privately held startup, touting letters of intent might be okay. It shows momentum. But as a public company, a letter of intent is not a sale. Eventually the shareholders or even the SEC are going to want to know where's the revenue. I started asking the client, and they ultimately agreed that there was some potential downside to calling a letter of intent a sale. If we hadn't pressed with tough questions to find the truth, they may well have been in trouble.

We saw in the 2016 election the ability of almost comically untrue stories and information to go viral to the point where you can start doubting there is an objective truth to a situation. That's a real concern, we seem to be drifting more and more into an environment Rudy Giuliani described with that stunning line. "The truth isn't truth." A real epitaph for our times.

One of the most frequent failures of truth are false and misleading claims. From greenwashing and wokewashing to inflating numbers, this is one of the most common ethical challenges.

Joe Cohen, APR, CCO of AXIS Capital, faced a challenge when the FDA questioned the truthfulness of KIND bars claiming to being *Healthy* when he worked there.

KIND was asked to remove the word *Healthy* from the label on several of its snack bars because of what we felt was an outdated guideline that just looked at the fat content in the product. The KIND bars in question were made of nuts that were high in good fats. It wasn't as well-known back in 1990 when the regulations were written that there were good fats and bad fats. Because of that, we were told that we had to take *Healthy* off the product.

We felt that was wrong. It was outdated guidance, and we decided to push back. We took pains to be very respectful and to push back in a way that was smart and strategic, but never contentious.

A small team worked on it. Our general counsel, the marketing team, and then comms and I had to report in to the CMO.

We worked 24/7 when the news broke. In high-pressure situations like that, you're exhausted because you're working round the clock, making decisions in real time, and you're doing it with very little sleep.

We developed a collaborative productive relationship with the FDA, and ultimately, they changed course and reversed that guideline. It wound up being not just a victory for KIND, but it also was a good example of how industry and government can work together to resolve differences in a productive manner.

Despite pros best efforts, eventually they will likely at some point unwittingly share false or incorrect information. **Janelle Guthrie**, APR, Fellow PRSA, of the Building Industry Association of Washington, discusses what to do in that situation:

My biggest ethical challenge came when I was working on a heated political campaign. I received a call from a reporter saying he'd heard my candidate had inflated his resume. The candidate's biography listed him as a commercial real estate broker. The tipster said that he hadn't achieved the credentials to be a broker. Not knowing the ins and outs of commercial real estate, I waited for him to come in and I asked him. He replied "I'm an agent. I've never been a broker." When we told him we've been calling him a broker he said, "Well, we should fix that."

I recommended issuing a media advisory saying we're fixing it in. We discussed whether we needed to do that. It's a good idea because people will understand there was a mistake, and we fixed it.

What I learned from that was to have the confidence to ask and don't assume. As an ethical advisor, a big part of our role is to question and clarify things. What sounded like a little thing, the difference between a real estate broker and a real estate agent, was actually a big deal to people who were brokers and had gone through the work to achieve that designation. Also, if you have a reputation of telling the truth and admitting when there are mistakes, then you receive more grace from the general public.

Moving from what you say to what you do—another common intentional failure of truth deals with expense reports. When you travel for a company, you invariably spend some of your own money because you forget to get a receipt. Some people turn to lying on their expense reports to make up for the loss. This is a global issue. **Hasan Zuberi,** President of the PR Council of Pakistan, explains:

> I remember what I used to do, like all my colleagues … if you're going to a client's office, we took the bus and we used to charge for the cabs. Our taxi fare cost 200 rupees, but a public bus only cost 20 rupees. I used to pocket those 180 rupees.
>
> But I realized it was not right. It wasn't limited to Pakistan. When I moved to the UAE, we had a procedure for submitting taxi company invoices. I submitted my taxi expenses as they really were and my HR exec called me and he said, "Your boss was not happy with you because he was charging a good double the amount for the same destination."
>
> But the executive told me to keep honesty as a trait. This has been a good practice that I started following, and still do today.

Lying on time sheets is another common casualty of the truth in agencies. **Darryl Salerno,** Owner of Second Quadrant Solutions, shares his experience:

> I know of many instances at other agencies where the time sheet was manipulated. Time must be logged exactly the way it was spent. There is a tendency to not want to go over budget and to move time from a budget that may be going over to a budget that has room on it. Even within the same client, that's not right. If one budget goes over and one budget is under, that's the way it is.
>
> Every hour must be logged exactly the way it was spent. When I was running my own agency, I would say, "And if anybody ever tells you differently, let me know because I will fire them on the spot." To me, the sanctity of the accuracy of the information that

goes into the system is critically important in terms of fairness to the client and employees getting credit for the time that they work.

These issues haven't changed since the 1970s. For some employees, it's hard to push back unless you know that top management within the company has a point of view on this. Problems come up when a manager feels that their career may be somewhat at risk if they blow a budget. It's important for top management to make it clear to the employees at all levels that that's not acceptable behavior.

There's also another aspect of this, and that's agencies have to be very careful about how they articulate problems with over-servicing. If you are giving someone a hard time about blowing a budget, some time won't get logged because people are afraid that they're going to look bad.

You have to accept that there are many causes to be over or under budget, because it's not a science, it's an art. Have the mindset of "I need to know, I need to understand, I need to get a handle on why we went over budget to not repeat those mistakes going forward."

If I'm at the top of the management chain, I want my managers to understand we'll work together and figure out how to solve the problem. You can't just say to an employee, "Listen, I gave you 30 hours to work on this this month" because if you tell them you gave them 30 hours, they're going to only log 30 hours.

But if you say to them, "I gave you 30 hours to work on this this month, but I may be wrong, you may need more than that. If you do, just let me know." That's a matter of language, but it's a whole different way that the employee has now been given permission to do what they need to do for the client, which is what's most critical.

Another common failure of truth is when PR professionals guarantee media coverage or overpromise. **Mike Neumeier**, APR, CEO of Arketi Group, explains:

I have worked under a few folks that made over-reaching promises as far as what an agency can do for a client. Those are always tricky situations, especially when you're early in your career and you've got a business owner that's all but guaranteeing something will happen. All you can do is work your butt off to try to make it happen.

In the PR world, we can't guarantee placements. We can't guarantee that an elite media outlet is going to take interest in a story, or that they're even going to sit down and have a cup of coffee with someone.

Beyond guaranteeing media coverage, some clients ask you to promote vaporware. **Cheryl Goodman,** former Head of Corporate Communication for Sony Electronics North America, explains how to avoid this:

Avoiding vaporware starts a year and a half before launch when there's an articulation of when it will come out. As you get closer to those launch timeframes and you start to see key features fall to the wayside, it's like, "Okay, we're aiming to meet a date. What's more important, meeting the date or meeting customers' expectations?"

This is a very legitimate conflict because *first to market* is a premium in perception and potentially revenue. The solution is finding a balance and calibrating expectations early and often. Working under embargo with a journalist, letting them know what your intent is, and maybe put less focus on whether it launches in the fourth quarter on the 31st at 11:59 p.m. to meet that deadline. It is calibrating expectations and being that voice of reason in the room.

It's not always a popular voice. The corporate communications person is always looking out for the greater good of the brand. Speaking generally, there's often conflict between product PR people and corporate communications. The product PR people are measured on success of the product, and corporate PR pros are measured on success of the brand.

You've got to be ready to negotiate and be the voice of reason.

It goes beyond vaporware. PR pros can often be asked to make absurd and misleading claims. **Ron Culp**, APR, Fellow PRSA, Director of Public

Relations and Advertising Master's Program at DePaul University, shares a delicious example:

> I was working at Sara Lee Corporation. Charlie Lubin, who founded the bakery, was a believer that everything had to be all natural, but there was a big push to create desserts that had fewer calories. Every time Sara Lee tried to come up with something that stayed true to all-natural ingredients but had fewer calories, it didn't taste good.
>
> We just kept working on it. Finally, they came up with this dessert that they labeled *Lite*, and we were asked to promote it through a public relations and marketing campaign.
>
> One day a reporter from the *New York Times* called our media person and asked her if she could give them some information about the product and its ingredients. We provided it and then he says, "Yes, but we had it tested and found that it had the same calorie content, even though it was labeled L-I-T-E."
>
> We went into a kind of a mini-crisis mode to find out what went on and found out from the division that it was indeed *lite* if you cut it in eight slices rather than six slices.
>
> It was a true OMG moment for those of us in the PR department. The head of media relations was told that we should respond by saying "It's lite, as in texture."
>
> My colleague simply said, "I just can't say that. That's just ridiculous. I'm going to look like a fool." My management team said, "Well, that's what our statement's going to be. So, you, Culp need to give that response."
>
> I did, and it had to be one of the most embarrassing quotes I've ever seen in my life. I got a lot of grief from other PR friends and media friends who said, "You've got to be kidding," which is exactly what the *New York Times* reporter said. But I was quoted as saying "It's lite as in texture." We didn't have much wiggle room to get out of it. If I could do it over again, I would never have been caught in that predicament.
>
> Never compromise your personal ethical standards. I knew my mother would look at me and say, "You're kidding," if I tried that

line with her. I felt awful after I hung up from the phone having said that. I should have pushed back and insisted on a different kind of response. The ensuing story made me look like a fool.

A few years later I joined the Arthur Page Society and fully embraced the seven Page Principles, especially the very first one, to tell the truth. From that day forward, it was so much easier.

The competition all had Lite products. The big difference is they tasted awful. Eventually we essentially threw up our hands and said, "People are buying our products because they taste good, and they're going to use them for special occasions."

If I had to do it again, I would have thrown myself into the data and the package literature, to understand exactly what this product contained. Instead, we just took everyone's word for the fact that it was lite, L-I-T-E. As a result, we got caught in this situation. If it sounds too good to be true or tastes too good to be true … it is.

Sometimes the client specifically asks you to lie for them. **Gini Dietrich**, the founder of SpinSucks, shares an example:

A few years ago, a client called me and said, "I know you have former journalists on staff. Could you have one of them call Governor's office and pretend that they're from the city newspaper, and see if you can get some information?"

And I was like, "No???"

He gave me a hard time about it. I had to sit down with him and explain why that wasn't ethical. He finally kind of got it. I don't think he totally agreed with me; I think to this day he doesn't think that there was anything wrong it. But he finally came around to if I want this done, it's not going to be through my PR firm.

Sometimes the lies are more insidious. **Marcy Massura,** CEO of MM & Company, faced a more difficult situation:

I had a prospect wanting to promote subscription sales on a SaaS solution, but they were planning on shuttering it. They were just trying to generate ending cashflow. The ethical question was where does my loyalty lay?

Anybody who knows me knows that I'm kind of a loudmouth. I'm not known as being subtle in any capacity. I immediately raised the red flag saying that this would put both my name and my company name in a bad light. Their claim was, you can just say that you didn't know. You can play stupid.

I said to them, "I don't ever want to be in a position where I have to defend my actions in that manner." The truth is, you don't get a chance to defend yourself. Once people think of you one way, that's the perception. There's no court of ethics. They mentioned that things can go away at any moment. Any client could be closing down and you may not know about it. So, it shouldn't matter.

The difference for me is I did know about it.

I respectfully declined the contract. However, I did recommend another individual who would do the work. You could say that that was a bit of an ethical compromise because I certainly wasn't on my moral high ground. It was kind of a middle ground.

Some clients may ask you to tell the truth, but to do it in a way that promotes fear. **Melanie Ensign**, the former Head of Security, Privacy, and Engineering Communications for Uber, advises against this:

There is a huge tendency in security and privacy to rely on FUD tactics (fear, uncertainty, and doubt). A lot of this comes from security companies trying to sell solutions.

To be fair, I've been in their shoes. I have done that. I understand the angst and why that feels like an obvious path. But we can do a better job educating our internal and external clients on why that is such a dangerous path if our goal is to protect people.

If you understand how the brain responds to that type of stimuli, then you understand that it's counterproductive. That is why, we see the same issues popping up over and over again in the data protection space. We are simultaneously trying to scare people while shoving new information at them. Psychologically, that's not how the cognitive mind works.

We have created this dangerous situation within the security space where the topic in general demobilizes a lot of people. They tune out. We have warning fatigue, because there are too many things coming at us at once. When people are scared of something, they're less likely to pay attention to it. It's hard for them to make good decisions. It's important to understand how the human brain actually responds to stimuli like that.

When I see someone going down this path of fear mongering, I know right away their number one priority is not actually protecting people. It's not all sunshine and rainbows, but you need to talk about risk in a way that's going to help people grasp the concept and to take action rather than make them run away or stick their head in the sand.

Rather than use FUD, we should liken it to the process of learning how to scuba dive. I am an avid scuba diver and a shark advocate. It is not natural for humans to breathe underwater. Every part of your body is avidly against this process. When you're starting out, there can be a lot of anxiety. Yet if we didn't teach and train people how to manage that risk and how to protect themselves, imagine all of the things that we would never know about the ocean?

It's just a matter of understanding, "Why are people are worried about this?" And recognizing that information and curiosity is the antidote to that.

If somebody is scared of something, it's usually because they don't understand it or because they're lacking information. I teach my teams to look at this as if we're teaching somebody to scuba dive. There are risks. We need to be honest about those risks, otherwise you might make a dangerous mistake. But if we fixate on that, we're never going to get them to the next step, which is helping them have a productive and enjoyable experience.

There's a security conference we host in Hawaii and every year. I started developing a dive track to help security engineers and security professionals get certified in scuba diving. I take them through that process with a dive master so that they now have a very recent experience of going through that fear.

They now personally understand what it is like to overcome that anxiety and the experience they had once they got to the other side. I tell them to pay close attention to things that the dive master is doing to help guide them through that learning experience.

In the world of cybersecurity, we have to be the dive masters. We are responsible for protecting people and teaching them what they can do to protect themselves.

Sometimes, it is people who work for you who demonstrate dishonesty and unethical behavior. **Ana Toro**, APR, Fellow PRSA, who works in communication for the CDC, shares an example from her work in another organization.

I was brought to lead a program and oversee the work of three subcontractors. I discovered two subcontractors were demonstrating unethical conduct and inappropriate behaviors.

They were not serving the best interests of the client. In my eyes, they were not following high standards of accuracy and truth. The subcontractor was not being truthful to the client on calls. So, after careful consideration, less than a week after I began the role, I had to fire one of the subcontractors.

My company and the contractor's officers were very scared about my decision, but I took a stand and walked them through it, with clear examples that supported my arguments. I even called former employees to gather additional history on the situation.

I was very honest with the team and told them what happened and why the decision was made. Tell them the why because you don't want this to continue.

It's not a decision that is often done in the company, because there's always concern, "There's going to be a lawsuit. Now they're going to come after us. They're not going to want to work with us anymore," but I was firm and convinced it had to happen.

My supervisor backed me, and we were able to do it. The decision proved to be the right decision when my client thanked me a few weeks later.

Intellectual Property

Intellectual property theft represents another common area of ethical failure for professionals with honesty at its core. **Elise Mitchell**, APR, Fellow PRSA, former Chairman of Mitchell Communications Group, explains:

A very common ethics challenge is the temptation to use other people's ideas. Lapses are far too common. You see it every day. It's so maddening. We've got to do a better job as an industry of respecting the ideas, words, and designs, everything that is inherent in somebody else's intellectual property.

The first time this came to light for me was when I was on the Cannes Lion PR Jury several years ago. The judges kept commenting to each other about, "Oh my goodness, I've seen this idea a hundred times." It finally came to a head about Day 2 because there was repetition of ideas from the past where somebody had taken a campaign and had just recreated it but tried to make it appear as though it was their own. It created a very intense discussion amongst us, as jurors, about what are the ethical standards we would expect people to live up to, globally.

As a group we said, "We're not going to accept it." I was proud of how our group took a very firm stand on this because there was some incredibly creative work that when we began to research it and think it through, we said, "Yes, but we've seen this idea done many times." But other people would say, "But there's not an original idea in the world."

What we decided, was, "You can't take an idea from your own industry and use it in sort of a blanket way to where it becomes clear that it was taken from somebody else." We wanted to challenge people to be original in their thinking. Now, you could take an idea from another industry, and put a different twist on it. This is a subtlety, but it's crucial, because this is a core part of the Code of Ethics for PRSA, you cannot take other people's ideas.

This begs the bigger questions of "What's original?" and "What are we allowed to use in terms of looking around at other very successful and cool ideas and using them in different ways?"

There is no original idea under the sun in terms of basic storylines. Those of us who are storytellers know that. There's nothing wrong with building off of a basic blueprint for putting a campaign together. Where you cross the line is when you begin using the nuances of other people's campaigns and ideas so blatantly that you begin to see it's a shadow of another campaign.

The key question you have to ask yourself is, "How do you put a truly unique twist on it, put your brand or client's fingerprints on it in a way that is authentic to them, but doesn't feel like a complete knockoff of something else?"

There isn't a shortage of ideas. The hardest part of an ideation session is turning the corner to say, "Okay, what are our two or three best out of the 320 ideas we've just come up with?"

That's where you have to stop and say, "Are we consciously or subconsciously using somebody else's idea? We should stop and check." That's where you challenge your creative process to go to the next level, based on a strategic insight that makes the idea authentically yours.

Bonnie Upright, APR, Vice President of Employee and Client Communications for Citi, shares an example of IP theft that struck very close to home.

My mother passed away in 2015 from pancreatic cancer, 29 days from diagnosis to death. She knew the day she was diagnosed; she was terminal. She went home, she sat down, she wrote her obituary. It was brilliant. I of course did my daughterly duties. I submit the obituary to the local newspaper here in Jacksonville.

She wrote every single word. It was wonderful. Because of the relationship I have as a PR person here in Jacksonville, a few of my media friends picked up on it, and *Times Union* did a story about the obituary and how great it was. Next thing you know … another friend whose husband happened to work at the *TODAY Show* saw it on my Facebook and saw the *Times Union* story. So suddenly it shows up on the *TODAY Show*. Well, once it shows up on the *TODAY Show*, *Good Morning America's* not far behind, and *CBS*, and all of them.

I hate the phrase went viral, but that's what happened. It went everywhere. I thought, well, this is kind of cool. My mom has kind of given me something to do, throughout the grief process. So, I immediately did what any good PR person does as the interview requests are coming in ... I set up a Dropbox with high-res images and captions, and I've got the obituary as a PDF, and in Word, so I can refer all of these editors and reporters.

A few months later, I'm sitting in the movie theater and a friend of mine texts me a story from a Richmond paper. It is a story saying how wonderful a particular woman's obituary was. Isn't this fantastic and great? I look at it, it's some older woman. She was 101, I think. Her picture next to my mother's words. Straight up, all of my mother's words.

I called my brother, and we realized that somebody had plagiarized the obituary, basically just changed out the names and dates. Very, very personal details. But everything else was there, the lede, the middle, the closing graph. All of it. It was crazy.

The night it happened I posted on the newspaper's Facebook page going, "Hey, this is kind of cool. But it was cool the first time when my mother wrote it back in Jacksonville," and shared a link. The next morning, I get up, I hadn't slept much that night. I call the newsroom at 8:15 in the morning and spoke with the assistant news editor. He said, we were just talking about you and were going to reach out to you. Will you do an interview with us? I said sure. I take the high road, of course ... my mother would want me to. "Isn't it flattering that someone loves your words so much, mom, that they took them for themselves?" Great, fine. My position was this woman was over a 100 years old. It wasn't as if they didn't know she was not going to be alive for much longer. They had time to write something. Right? You've had time to write something.

Honestly, the bleeding heart in me also was very much, "This mom deserved her own story." Everyone has their own story.

Within another month or so, it happens again. Then it happens again. Montana, similar situation. I get a hold of the family, they cry, they apologize. They play the Montana card, "We just live in Montana. Nothing like this ever happens in Montana. We didn't know it was going to be viral. We didn't know the newspaper would pick up on it." I'm like of course they're going to pick up on it. What are you doing? So, they apologize and we move on.

Since then, it has been plagiarized 14 or 15 times now, either in whole or in part. There's a paragraph in the middle where my mother talks about her grandchildren. She said, "My greatest treasures call me Nana," and she talks about them. The last paragraph, the part about, "You can look for me in the daffodils, you can look for me in the butterflies." There are certain things that clearly resonate with folks. So, I try to track them down as best I can.

I know my mother would probably say, "Bonnie, just get over it. Don't worry about it." But for me and my brother, that was my mother's last love letter to her family. It's very personal. She sat up in bed at hospice and read it to us a few days that week before she died.

Please don't use my mother's words. Those were words that were meant for us, and special for us. But again, this whole thing of, "Well, it was on the Internet, so I must be able to take it." It's like when people lift photos from online, with no attribution or anything. All I ask for is simple attribution, and sometimes I get it, and sometimes I don't.

If I don't, I just let it go. Who has time to chase them all down? But I do have Google alerts set up on all these various phrases. That's how I find them, or someone will say, "Oh my gosh, here's another one."

The stories are crazy though. There was an Illinois one, it turned out to be a meth head. The family started arguing because they said, "Aunt X never would have never written this, she was a meth head. This doesn't sound like her." Then a columnist got a hold of the story. I mean, this is crazy town, but what are you going to do?

If for some reason you can't get a hold of someone for permission, at the very least give attribution. It doesn't take away from your blog post, or from your image. Now if you start using it to make money, that is a whole different thing, attribution ain't going to cover your ass there, that's for sure.

But Holy Moly. Don't steal, people. Don't steal.

Other Examples

Judy DeRango Wicks, APR, Fellow PRSA and former communications lead for Fiserv, shares an example of how she ethically addressed a situation when she could benefit from misinformation around their online billing technology:

After 9/11, someone was mailing anthrax in envelopes through the postal system. It seemed like 200 reporters had the same idea at the same time. They called me to say, "Isn't this going to be great for online bill pay? Are you seeing a surge of adoption?"

There was temptation to say "Yes, we're seeing a surge in adoption," but it wasn't true. We understood behavior well enough to know that we probably would not, because fear was not what led people to pay their bills online.

We relied on data to make sure we were being accurate. We were doing lots of research, so we were excruciatingly knowledgeable about bill pay behavior and different types of people, and their attitudes toward paying bills.

This was before social media, but it was a wildfire story. Everybody was covering the anthrax story. I could've jumped into that by saying what these reporters kept asking me 50 different ways trying to get me to say, "We're getting a surge."

As a public company, that would be unethical and a bad idea. When earnings came around, investors would ask about the surge. We had to step back and think how are we going to respond to these inquiries? With the help of our agency, we decided that we would participate in positive stories that talked about all the good things about bill pay that would truly drive adoption—that you save time, that you're protected by a guarantee, you have a record of payments, and so on.

We had the agency filter these inquiries. If it sounded like they wanted to do a story about fear of anthrax, we would decline participation. But if a reporter said *yes*, they would do a thorough story about bill pay and how to get started, and all those things that could lead us to having people try it, then we would do those interviews. We sacrificed many articles.

It was the right thing to do. We ended up with some perfect stories. The *USA Today* story was so perfect that I framed it and put it on the wall. It said exactly what we had intended.

Also, we did not see the wisdom in associating our brand with anthrax, of all things. Why would I want a sentence that had my company name connected with anthrax? So, we avoided being associated with anthrax when we were barely getting started becoming a known brand.

A few weeks later. I was at the PRSA International Convention, and I'm sitting next to the head of PR for Hallmark Cards, and we had an interesting conversation—the same reporters were calling her trying to get her to say, "Are people afraid of sending Christmas cards this year?" It was interesting to see firsthand that they were trying to put the quote in our mouth, and we had to resist to keep that from happening.

Honesty and Ethics Advice

It is not all negative. **Paul Omodt**, APR, Fellow PRSA, the principal of Omodt and Associates, discusses how honesty repairs reputations:

> I've worked with individuals and brands who've done unethical things. I tell them after the apology, you have to work from the inside out. I'll actually throw a rock in a puddle of water and have them watch the ripples go out. We'll identify those closest people that they need to go reach out to.
>
> There's a theory of communications that says the people that are hurt the most, deserve the closest, most personal communication. I have those people reach out personally to those people and have a conversation. That's a very difficult conversation to have. It will

stress them out. But once they do it, they feel slightly less bur-
dened by their emotions and then they move onto the next one
and the next one and the next one.

I had a client who had used the N word when he was younger.
It was captured on a video tape that surfaced 20 years later. It cost
him his high-profile job.

He said, that is something I said in that moment when I was
19 years old. Now I'm a 40-year-old man. I need to own that. He
went out to all the people who have been impacted by that and
then all the churches in the area. He slowly worked his way back
up and literally five years later, he got appointed back to that post
because people saw real contrition.

But it was a step-by-step process of apologizing both personally or in letters or in group settings, it was a very metered out. The
clients that I work with on situations like that feel better about it
over time, and they feel like a more complete person.

Mark Dvorak, APR, Fellow PRSA, Executive Director of Golin
Atlanta, also sees how consistent honesty helps when you make a mistake:

I was blessed to have the chance to be around Al Golin and listen
to him for years before he passed away. Al was the brains and
thought leader behind the *Trust Bank*. About how everything
comes down to trust and doing the right things on an everyday
basis and building relationships so that when you have a challenge, folks are more likely to support you … or at least give you
the benefit of the doubt.

Today, the biggest threat to ethical behavior for PR practitioners is fake news. I'm sitting here watching the hearing on the
whistleblower complaint with the White House and thinking,
"Wow." We have as a society screwed up the idea of what's a fact
and what's not a fact. It's an issue for public relations as it creates
more of this gray area in our jobs. It's a slippery slope. We've got
to do something about it.

Fortunately, I was a double major in communications and history. When you study history, you realize that a lot of things are

cyclical in the world. What allows me to sleep at night is the fact that I believe we as a profession and society are going to react powerfully enough that the pendulum is going to swing back to the other side. There's a reason you have multiple sources. There's a reason you'd have three editors reviewing and fact checking.

Col. Ann Knabe, PhD, APR+M, U.S. Air Force, discusses the threat of disinformation and dishonest information being spread about companies:

What bristles me is how writers are associating disinformation with public relations. One article from a national outlet[2] had a headline that said, "Disinformation for hire. How a new breed of PR firms is selling lies online" and called the rise of disinformation, black PR. That's not how I perceive our profession.

I'm trying to be really clear when I'm saying *dis*, with a D. Disinformation is different from misinformation, with an M. Disinformation is false information, intended to mislead. Disinformation is very deliberate, very purposeful. It is deception to distribute untrue material that's intended to influence public opinion.

Disinformation has become easier to spread with social media. But disinformation is rooted in the Russian term dezinformatsiya. Looking back at the 1920s, the Soviet Union was using fake or false information as a weapon. Later, we saw it pop-up during the Cold War. But in the last couple of years, where I've observed this is the spread of fake news is on social media, with that very deliberate intent of being deceptive. With the rise of automated and artificial intelligence, fake social media accounts, and fake news sites, disinformation can now get more traffic generated more quickly than a human could.

The sad part about it is a lot of these sophisticated technologies are being used to target real people. They're using the sophisticated algorithms of Facebook and other social media that initially

---

[2] C. Silverman. January 06, 2020. Buzzfeed. www.buzzfeednews.com/article /craigsilverman/disinformation-for-hire-black-pr-firms.

were very good things, but now can be used in a very nefarious way. These algorithms are affecting what shows up on your feeds and can be used to manipulate vulnerable people.

It's very difficult to stay ahead of this. It's almost impossible. But I insist the firms doing this are not public relations firms. It's contrary to what our profession stands for, and it's contrary to the PRSA Code of Ethics.

Quentin Langley, Author of *Brandjack*, highlights issues with honesty and brandjacking:

It is so easy to create blatantly false statements about organizations. I wrote in my last book, *Brandjack*,[3] about a Twitter trend, "Seriously McDonald's?" that was a Photoshop sign in a McDonald's window saying that they were going to charge more to African American customers. It was untrue, but it went all over Twitter. I think that reflects what a lot of people think about McDonald's. There are lot of brands, like Whole Foods, where no one would've taken it seriously.

Responding to untrue allegations can be challenging. It depends on the reservoir of goodwill that brands already have. For McDonald's, there is a lot of hostility to the brand. There are a lot of people who like the brand as well, but it seems to me that a lot of McDonald's customers view it in a very transactional way. It's not a brand that they feel loyal to. So, for McDonald's, handling that is very difficult.

Then there's the issue if someone within your organization shares a tweet of fake news or any number of stupid conspiracy theories. How does the organization deal with that? If the CEO finds out that someone who works for the organization has shared a tweet saying, "Coronavirus as a hoax." How do you deal with that? Do you fire the person for sharing that tweet? Well then, we go back to this freedom of speech issue and say, "Well, that's his view, he's not speaking on behalf of the organization."

---

[3] Q. Langley. 2014. *Brandjack*, Springer.

It has to be a case-by-case judgment. How senior is the person, how associated is the person with the brand? If you're using the brand's Twitter feed, then that crosses a line immediately, and it doesn't matter who you are. If it is a very senior person with within an organization who is strongly associated with the brand, it potentially crosses a line.

Author Peter Shankman reminds us we do not need to be perfect:

Even though in today's political climate, lying has been almost approved—we need to understand that's not actually the case. You will get caught.

That's what amazes me about this world that we're in right now. Everyone thinks it's okay to lie, and they don't think they're going to get caught. It's so easy to get caught. The key is we have a much shorter attention span, so we don't care that much anymore, but there are people who do.

Because the bar is so ridiculously low, when it comes to what we expect from companies, we don't need to be awesome. We just need to suck a little less than normal.

If we expect everyone to suck, then I don't need a brand to be great. I just need them to understand that they could be a little bit better. If it comes down to an ethical dilemma that you're facing, doing the right thing is going to pay off.

Five Key Takeaways

How do we maintain the highest standards of truth and advocacy?

1. Remember the truth will always come out eventually.
2. Trust but verify.
3. Always give proper attribution.
4. Avoid wokewashing and greenwashing.
5. Fight disinformation. It is one of the greatest threats to public discourse and communication.

CHAPTER 4

Expertise

Using our expertise ethically is core to serving our employers and society well. I tell my students at Boston University—when you graduate, you will have superpowers to change opinions and drive action. You need to decide if you are going to use them for good or for evil. This chapter looks at challenges many professionals faced—and how they responded by using their powers for good.

The PRSA Code of Ethics states:

> *Expertise*: "We acquire and responsibly use specialized knowledge and experience. We advance the profession through continued professional development, research, and education. We build mutual understanding, credibility, and relationships among a wide array of institutions and audiences."

Expertise takes many forms. Following are challenges, advices, and failures of expertise.

Ethical Expertise Advice

Gary McCormick, APR, Fellow PRSA, a past President of PRSA, owns his own consulting firm, and previously worked in marketing and public relations for Scripps Networks Interactive, the parent company of cable network HGTV. He has great counsel on what to do when you encounter unethical behavior:

> Every day is a learning experience. Every community is different, every technology is different, every client is different. A key lesson I learned is at the end of the day, I have to truly believe what I'm saying. I have to be willing to question authority, especially in the

environmental area, because people's lives, health, and well-being could possibly be at risk. If you take that away from them, you can't give it back.

You can't recover your own reputation if you're caught supporting a falsehood or inaccuracy from your client or your cause. The end does not justify the means in this type of work, so I learned to ask:

- What do you know?
- When did you learn about it?
- Who did you tell about it?
- What did you do about it?
- How can we improve the situation?

I learned to say those things before I ever left the client's office and started interacting with the public. If they aren't comfortable with those answers or you aren't comfortable with those answers, then you need to make the change and move on, because if you can't get the absolute truth about where things are and what's known, if it comes out later, you have lost your reputation, and you've lost your ability to do the job for them.

This same process works well for managing people and being a parent.

Kami Huyse, CEO, Zoetica, highlights how expertise allows us to respond and not react to unethical behavior:

First of all, protect yourself first. That's number one.

If you encounter an unethical situation, get an ally. The ally could be somebody in your company, but it's usually not. It's usually somebody who is a good sounding board.

I always talk about responding, not reacting. If you react to abuse that makes you look like, "There's that crazy woman again." I like the idea of responding, which takes time. Think about what you're going to do. Make a plan and then execute that plan.

If you need to have legal help, get legal help. If you need to stand up for yourself in a more constructive way, do it. Somebody needs to stand. It's not easy. But it's necessary.

Michael Meath, the retired Interim Chair of public relations at the S.I. Newhouse School at Syracuse University, believes taking the "Critical 10" helps you make more ethical decisions.

People believe speed has to be instantaneous because that's the way the world works. I don't believe that. I'm an old dinosaur. Yes, we need to be quick. Yes, every moment that we hold off on saying something can hurt us or at least make people wonder whether we know anything. But that has to be balanced with taking the Critical 10, where you're figuring out and assessing what else is going on.

So, take the Critical 10, whether it's 10 seconds or 10 minutes, to get a sense of what's going on in the world.

Nicky McHugh, Global Head of Content for Rep Trak, agrees:

A former boss' words resonate with me still today. "Practice the pause," It took me a lifetime to learn this, and it's something I try to do frequently. It's the space between thoughts, the space between words, that space is where I find grace when in conflict, inspiration under stress, and inner peace when I simply give myself up to being open and vulnerable. Practice the pause.

Jim Lukaszewski, APR, Fellow PRSA, one of America's most respected crisis and ethics counselors, believes expertise is essential:

I wrote a book about expertise *Why Should the Boss Listen to You?*[1] It talks about what CEOs look for and what they want us to do for them.

---

[1] J. Lukaszewski. 2008. *Why Should the Boss Listen to You? The Seven Disciplines of the Trusted Strategic Advisor,* Jossey-Bass.

The first thing they want is advice on the spot. Business operates in real time. Bad things happen in real time. If you go to a meeting at 10:00 and are debriefed, and then you leave and try to figure out what you do, and you come back at 2:00 … a lot has happened in those four hours and you're forcing the management to go back. Which they'll do, probably with great courtesy, and then they don't do what you suggest because they're past the information point that you give.

Another weakness we have is that we believe so strongly in what we believe that sometimes we don't realize how much pressure we're putting on people when we ask them to do things.

I have a 10-day rule on ideas. If they don't do it in 10 days, ask again if you think it's that important. But if they don't do it after that, drop it and move on to something else. They're not going to do it. They're adults. They have made the decision not to do it, and they're just too courteous to tell you get off it.

I spoke to one guy at a convention, and he said he couldn't get his manager to do what he proposed. I said, well, how long have you been proposing this kind of stuff? He said it's going on 13 years, 13 years! Does the manager even talk to you anymore?

Here's the problem. We tend to forget whose bus we are on. It's their bus. If you have a problem with how they're behaving or acting, get off the bus. Get another bus or start your own. Staff functions are paid to help management drive the bus better from their perspective.

There is a specific technique for giving expert advice that will be listened to. It's called a three-minute drill. It revolves around the concept of making suggestions and writing options for action. Always have three potential options for them to choose from. Our problem is we're so strong on communication that we walk in, and the boss wants options, but we say things like, I know in my heart this is the right thing to do. Well, the boss isn't running the bus with his heart.

We characterize ourselves as solution finders. But many of us can't be solution finders because we can't add, subtract, multiply, or divide. The rest of management can. The solution I have found over the past 25 years is to offer three options every time. The three options are very simple.

First is to do nothing, and it is a strategic option. We tend to avoid it because we like to do stuff, but doing nothing is a zero percent solution. Then there's doing something, which I call the 100 percent solution, which is important to do, and then there's the third category, which I call doing something more—or the 125 percent option.

Always give them three choices. This is the one time perhaps in our entire career when they recognize that we were thinking about their problems from their perspective. They will like it, and they will call you back sooner.

Offer options instead of solutions because options are smaller, they're doable and you're actually helping them be successful. People who do this notice they get called back sooner than others.

One of the mistakes we make when there's trouble is staff people link arms around the people in trouble and want to keep all the other voices away. This is the one time in a boss's life when they want to talk to anybody for any reason who might have any information on how to solve this thing. The people who are listened to, including public relations people, are the ones who help them find people to talk to. Particularly in the crisis arena, they want to talk to everybody.

One thing I've learned in my career is people do not change. We can coach them incrementally to improve things. But if it's illegal, immoral, monumentally stupid, and irritating, you're going to have to change jobs. You're going to have to go someplace else. If you have good advice and they're not taking it, find a place that will.

Fred Cook, former Chairman of Golin and Director of the USC Center for Public Relations, expands on how to be an expert counselor:

To be an effective counselor, you must be in touch with the values of your client or your agency. The more that you can codify your behavior in advance, the easier it is to make a decision when something happens, because you know immediately if this is a good thing or a bad thing or how we're going to respond. Second, you must find out all the information as quickly as you can. Sometimes, these issues get prolonged and aggravated because the people communicating about them don't know the full story in the beginning, and they have to keep retelling it over and over as the information comes out.

Oftentimes, with a sticky issue, you're better off resolving it as quickly as you can. It means that people in communications have to understand what is at stake in a conversation about gun control, or a conversation about climate change, or a conversation about immigration. These are very complicated topics, and employees are asking companies what their stand is. Customers want to know what the organization believes about these topics.

It's not just enough to know about communications. You've got to understand everything you can about these individual issues, and many of them are quite complex and have very compelling stories on both sides. As you look at the current debate about Roe versus Wade, this is going to be something that companies are going to be asked to take a stand on. These are very complex and very emotional issues, and it requires a great sense of knowledge and a keen sense of judgment on the part of the people who communicate about them.

Expertise Ethics Issues in Action

Dave Close, the former managing director of MSL Boston, provides counsel on how to tell a client they are being unethical:

> We had a hard charging client who asked us to call their competitors using fake names and fake company names to gather competitive intelligence. It was pretty easy to say, "No we're not going to do that." It's certainly legitimate for companies to gather competitive intelligence, and they can do it themselves or they can hire companies that do that. But I just didn't like the idea of using fake names as a PR agency working for this company. There was

quite a bit of grumbling, but when I explained why we couldn't, he understood, and he relented.

There was a legitimate chance that the agency could have been fired. At one point this client said "Well why did I hire you guys? What am I paying you guys for?" I said, "You're paying us to do honest PR. Being clear about our affiliation and our role, not calling people with fake names." I think that this client thought about firing us, but I believe he liked the work that the agency team was doing for him and ultimately was not going to fire us over that.

There's a great line from Thoreau that stuck with me: "Beware of all enterprises that require new clothes."[2] I would also say to PR people beware of all endeavors that require fake names. That's just not the business we're in. And it's not how we operate.

You're not going to have much of a business for long if you do dishonest things. In today's world of social media and Google, if you're dishonest, it is going to come out. Then not only are you dishonest, but you're also recognized for being dishonest, and that's going to hurt any kind of business.

It is essential to just say something more than "That's unethical" when providing expert counsel around ethical issues. **Marisa Vallbona,** Founder and President of CIM, Inc. PR, provides advice on why we need to use our expertise to dig deeper:

A member of a client's organization asked me to do something that was clearly unethical. We were having cocktails with one of the managers with this client's organization, and the member looked at me over martinis and asked me to do something that was unethical. I was actually pretty shocked.

The reason that this was such a stressful dilemma is because this client means so much to me. It's a substantial client for me. The manager looked at this individual and said, "She can't do that.

---

[2] H.D. Thoreau. n.d. *Walden.*

She's an APR. She's a Fellow. She will lose her credentials. Not only that, it's illegal."

I sat there and I thought, I operate offices in Southern California and in Texas. All of a sudden, I can see myself just leaving Southern California going to Texas, having to resign this client and just being done with it because I can't do this. I was so happy that the manager protected me.

But here is the thing that I thought was really interesting, and this is a lesson for all of us. The member who was asking me to do something completely unethical is a very ethical person. I don't think this individual realized what they were really asking me to do.

After cocktails, I thought about it for a while and I thought, what was behind this? What was this individual's pain? Where did this request come from? What was this person's end game? What was gnawing at them and keeping them up at night?

When I realized what their pain was, I was able to come up with a workaround that was ethical, that was legal, and I was able to solve their problem while maintaining ethics and legality. What we can all learn from this is sometimes clients, employers, and organizations might ask us to do something that is shocking and comes across as unethical, but they're not necessarily coming at it from that perspective. We need to take a step back and understand what is their goal. What exactly do they want?

Kelley Chunn, Principal of Kelley Chunn and Associates, shared how she uses her expertise to determine if organizations that make mistakes on race and systemic injustice deserve help.

There was an educational institution that was in the middle of a crisis around a letter of solidarity that they had sent out to their stakeholders.

There was pushback about the content of the letter. While the letter attempted to communicate a feeling of solidarity in response to George Floyd's murder, the letter seemed to be more concerned about supporting law enforcement than it did about police brutality and violence. It threatened to become a full-blown issue.

I talked to a friend about this who is not in the business about whether or not I should help. She said, "Well, why would you help them out? They got in trouble. It's really their issue. Why should you try to bail them out?"

She saw it as an ethical issue. I saw it as a practitioner, and that they needed help. They realized that they've made a mistake, that they could have said this in a more empathetic manner, so why not help them out? We looked at it very, very differently, but she made me think about what I was doing and why I was doing it.

There are some clients who come to me about projects, and I would rather not take them on and I will decline. I could have done so in that instance, but I felt that their intentions had been good, and they just needed some help.

I realized that time was of the essence. We had to act fast, act truthfully, and act first. It requires asking the right questions.

- What have you been doing with regard to diversity and inclusion?
- How can you communicate that to your stakeholders?
- Who's on your board?
- Who have you hired?
- Who is teaching?
- Who is in senior management?

I had them answer those questions as they communicated with their stakeholders.

Businesses need to demonstrate what, if anything, that they've already done, outlining a plan for the future that includes hiring and promotion and board composition.

Garland Stansell, APR, Chief Communications Officer for Children's of Alabama, encountered a situation where it wasn't his company that had an issue, but could be found guilty by association:

We were constructing a new expansion facility. One morning, we had protesters on the construction site because one of the contractors had a history of using undocumented individuals. We had meetings with the contractors, our board, and the hospital leadership, looking at what do we need to do about this? We had legal saying we haven't done anything wrong. It's up to the general contractor and the subcontractor who was employing undocumented individuals.

We said that kind of response does not fit. We were still in the midst of a recession, and we were one of the only projects in the state of Alabama of this magnitude.

That raised the visibility around the state. We needed to be proactive on this. We needed to come back and say we were not aware of this, and that we are demanding that this subcontractor verify that everyone that they have on their site is a citizen. If there was someone on the job site that was undocumented, that they were released from the job site, and replaced with someone who was either a naturalized citizen or a U.S.-born citizen.

We decided on the steps and the strategy on the first day, but it took about a week for it to blow over. I firmly believe that if we had not taken that stance and not held the contractor's feet to the fire and asked for those assurances from the subcontractor, that it would have gone on for much longer, and it could have grown to be even larger.

That was an ethical dilemma. Legally we had not done anything wrong. It was something that one of the subcontractors had done in the past, but you're guilty by association, and you need to consider what that looks like for your brand and your organization and your values as a company.

Ethics Issues in Media Relations

To pitch or not to pitch? That is the question. **Adam Blacker,** Vice President of Insights and Alliances at Apptopia, shares his insight on when to use your expertise to know when to ethically pass on a media opportunity:

I often have to use my expertise to make the decision to pass up on an opportunity for media coverage. Which, as a PR person, it's like, "How could you ever pass that up?" But because our data might not necessarily fit, I pass what could be a juicy narrative.

Why? In the long haul, I want to be a trusted source of data, and I don't want to mislead people. When we say something, I want them to be able to believe it. I want them to know we mean it, and that we stand behind it.

Our competitors will sometimes jump on something where they've taken advantage of setting parameters. Maybe they carefully selected the timeframe of the data to tell a story. For example, when COVID-19 started, certain European countries like Spain and Italy went into lockdown. Our competitors secured media coverage on the rise of streaming services.

They were saying, "There's an increase in downloads for Netflix in these countries this week versus the week prior." That's true. Our data picks up on that as well. It sounds like a reasonable item to push out. I could have gotten media coverage on that potentially. But we decided we're not going to release anything on it because it became clear after looking at the data that the increase was actually just part of the natural ebb and flow of downloads in that country. If you looked at a longer traunch, you couldn't pin it to the pandemic. I just didn't feel good about saying that this caused this, because if you just zoom out a little more than one week, it wasn't justified.

Anytime you look into data you have to just go, "What's happening." And then you have to zoom out and go, "How significant is this? Is it best ever, worst ever? Is it just for this period?" You've got to nail down the specifics when you're working with data.

It's easy to say, "I've got this data, I'm going to frame it like this, send it to a reporter." Most good reporters won't be fooled. But we won't even try. In certain situations, we will actively make the decision to not put it out there because we don't feel like it's substantial enough, or we don't feel like we can pin it to an event that happened.

You need to use your expertise. Play the long game because trust is everything. Once trust is eroded, it's hard to gain it back. With data being very accessible these days, people can find out pretty easily. Invest in yourself, invest in your company, invest in the stock market. It's smarter to play the long game.

Bryan Scanlon, the founder of Look Left Marketing, explains what he does when his client wants to speak out on an area in which they are not qualified or appropriate:

> I faced this issue around 9/11. There were some clients who said "We're in the security business. We need to be on television right now, because we believe it's going to be a cyberattack next. They're going to come after the critical infrastructure. We believe this is just the beginning."
>
> In retrospect, the answer seems easy. But, like all ethical dilemmas, in the moment, it's a little difficult. You're running pretty high on emotion. We always looked for opportunities to get clients on television. We often took risks and tried to seize moments. That debate did not last long in my head. The answer was, "No. You really can't do this."
>
> I asked every single one of those people. "Are you an expert in terrorism? Because those are the people who will provide value in this moment. Are you an expert in building design, construction, and safety? Then you could be of value to the public and to journalists."
>
> This notion of fear mongering, which exists a lot with security even today, was just not right. One client was like, "Well, you work for me. You should just do what I tell you to do." And I said, "Well, we can NOT work for you. You can't do this." And that was the first time that I ever uttered those words of, "We could not work for you" and say I am willing to walk away, because this is a line I'm not going to cross.

September 11 also created an ethics moment for **Martin Waxman**, APR:

> I was promoting Olay Daily Facials. We were trying to come up with a travel program for them to say, "Hey, these are great on the go."

The concept was, we had our media materials printed to look like old school boarding passes. We got metal school lunchboxes and had stickers put on them—New York City, Twin Towers, Paris, and London. We put a water bottle in there, product samples, and a few other goodies, and we sent them to media on September 10, 2001, thinking that this was kind of a cute, creative outreach.

9/11 happens, and we start getting calls from a dozen of the outlets saying, "You sent us a metal package. You've gotta deal with this. You gotta come pick it up because we cannot open it. We don't know what it is."

We quickly called our key media. They appreciated it because the worst thing is so many communications people don't empathize with media. We think of media as media and not as people. As soon as you put yourself in that position, you go, "Oh." That reshapes what my decision would be and helps give me another perspective.

We then had to figure out: How do we explain this to our client? We had to determine how to tell our client we were canceling the campaign and get them onboard and deal with the expenses we incurred for the agency.

We came up with an amicable financial solution for all of us, recognizing that we had done some work. We would have to make an investment, as our client did, but we built our client's trust by saying, "We cannot do this. In fact, we probably can never go out with this pitch again. We thought it was a great idea two weeks ago; because of what happened in the world, it's no longer appropriate, so we need to think of something else."

You've got to listen to your gut when it comes to ethics, and then you need a system to be able to cross-check to make sure that you're making the right decision. You need a process in place. You need to figure out if you are going to go with duty-based or a utilitarian-based approach.

Expertise, Ethics, and Research

Another area where expertise comes into play is with research. While this also has elements of transparency—the expertise of in-person research issues highlighted by **Robin Schell**, APR, Fellow PRSA, and **Stacey Smith**, APR, Fellow PRSA, Senior Counsel and Partners at Jackson, Jackson & Wagner, stands out.

Robin: We would work on controversial issues like landfill expansions. Those are not the most popular thing. Sometimes I would go into the communities, and just do some underground research. Just literally sit at some of the cafes and the popular spots in town, talk to people about how they felt about the landfill expansion that had been proposed. Get their gut reactions without telling them that I was actually representing the landfill. If they asked me, would I tell them? Absolutely. But I didn't necessarily present myself that way because I wanted to get an unbiased reaction from them.

I could have been a little bit more transparent about that. This was many, many years ago. Today it's a lot more acceptable to go out there in a very transparent way, and introduce yourself as, "Hey, I'm interested on behalf of XYZ company. They really want to know what you think."

Stacey elaborates: On the flip side, we were simply being sponges to hear what public opinion, what individuals were thinking on a subject. We weren't advocating, we weren't pushing any particular message. We just wanted to hear, and that's a form of research. Today, research is getting harder and harder because people either don't want to share anything or they want to share everything.

I'm a little worried about the ethics of where our research is going to go to try and understand our publics in such a way that is truly done in an ethical way. Right now, there are so many polls about this and that out there that you know they're not being done in a statistical fashion. That's unethical. For example, my local paper is running a survey, "Call in and tell us how you feel about X." And they get a hundred responses, and they're putting it out there as fact, that 75 percent said this. It's the worst poll. We're going to have to focus on the ethics of how to do good, honest, ethical research going forward.

Stacey: To do good ethical research, go find a good research course. Learn from the professionals how to conduct good research, how to pick a good sample that's balanced, how to ask questions that are not leading, how to look at data in a way that is truly honest in terms of how you're interpreting that data. Even if you're not going to be the one that's actually doing the research, you will have the skills to be able to look at research that you are buying, and know that it is done in a good, ethical fashion.

Even with qualitative research, don't start an internal project without making them commit to the fact that the data will be fed back to those who we are asking, so that they get that feedback of what's been said. You always run into these organizations that say, "Oh we did this, and then they put it in the bottom drawer. We never heard about it again." We won't do that. That's an ethical piece for us, where if they won't commit to that, we won't do the project.

Johna Burke, Global Managing Director for AMEC, elaborates and explains how agencies are using data incorrectly and not showing their expertise.

The biggest thing in public relations measurement is putting forward a number as ROI. We have diluted the financial term of ROI so much to twist it onto the P&L that over the years, whether it's ad value equivalency (AVE), reach, impressions, or some other number, we try to get tied to some single metric that isn't ROI.

Time and time again, you're talking about return on relationships, return on those efforts. You can talk about the correlation.

It has evolved because edge computing has created a means for a lot of organizations to build their own data stack so that it's getting them to a number that is their own net promoter internal scorecard, but it's using multiple data inputs that they're able to get to that point. If you're going to a single source and if you aren't giving that other costing data and they're presenting you something as ROI, it should be questioned at every turn.

We need to focus on the objectives that look at impact not output. An agency should not take an objective of increased awareness. They should focus on SMARTER objectives.

SMARTER Objectives

- Specific
- Measurable
- Attainable
- Realistic
- Time-bound
- Ethical
- Revolutionizing

There's a whole love affair with the biggest numbers, and as the data mix continues to evolve, those numbers are shifting all over the place. We've all heard the story of 11 billion impressions, yet you couldn't walk outside of your door and find one person who knew what happened. Is that realistic? Is that something that you want to have your name attached to? No.

Make sure that you are taking a measured and strategic approach. The more you ask the *Why*, you become a better, more trusted counselor.

Improving Ethical Expertise

Melanie Ensign, former Head of Security, Privacy, and Engineering Communications for Uber, explains how expertise changes your focus to stopping fires before they begin, rather than responding to a crisis:

People tend to glorify firefighting in our profession. That unfortunately leads a lot of communications professionals to think that they're most valuable when there's a crisis.

The reality is, we are incredibly valuable prior to that moment by helping our organization build muscle memory and resiliency so that they're better prepared to do the right thing when one of these big moments happens. Quite honestly, there's a lot that we can do to steer our organizations in a better direction so we can avoid some of these minefields. For me, that has been the most challenging ... making sure that I'm identifying some of these decisions that may seem innocuous right now but are just another step in boiling a frog. It is working to make sure that we don't actually end up in a position where we don't expect to be, just because we weren't careful about our choices early on.

One of the reasons why I feel like this is the most challenging and difficult is this is where you get a lot of the internal politics in an organization. You must be willing to stand up every single day for what the right thing is. That is a lot harder for most communications professionals in our organizations compared to when a crisis is happening, and everybody looks at the PR person for an answer. You have to make sure that you're able to insert your voice and to represent that consciousness of the organization on a daily basis, and with all of the teams that you work with regularly.

Helio Fred Garcia, President of Logos Consulting Group, agrees:

Structures and clear protocols make courage less necessary in ethical dilemmas. In the case of the first job that I had to resign from, the PRSA Code of Ethics is very clear that PR people may not make promises for things over which they have no control, including the specificity of foreseeable press coverage because we don't make the editorial judgment. I could say, "It's not me. And, by the way, at the bank, you have a regulatory duty to not speak materially misleading things." Pointing to structure is in many ways liberating because it isn't personal preference.

But if you have a legal duty that conflicts with your ethical duty, which do you choose, and how do you determine which to choose? That's actually not an easy decision. But the clearer you are about the criteria, the more likely you are to make the right choice.

For example, I teach in my engineering ethics course that Apple was ordered by a U.S. federal court to invent software that Apple believed would put millions of people's safety and security at risk.

Apple had to decide whether to abide by the law, which would put it in violation of the first ethical standard for engineers, which is to protect public safety, or abide by their ethical obligation to protect public safety but then be at risk of the full force of the U.S. government coming down upon them, including severe financial sanction.

When I ask my students, especially students from outside the United States who were not here when this happened five years ago, what do you think Apple chose? The answer I always hear is, "Oh, they chose to pretend to invent the software but not succeed," or, "Oh, they chose to invent the software and say they had no choice. The courts made them."

Apple chose to defy the court order. When Tim Cook, the CEO, went out to defend the decision, he said, "We have to stand tall and to stand tall on principle. And the principle is our first duty is to protect our customers. Everything else is secondary to that." That clarity helps you make the tough choices at the moment you need to make those choices.

Torod Neptune, former Chief Communications Officer at Lenovo, highlights how communication expertise can help move companies from the organization they are today to the one they want to be:

The most significant role and responsibility that I and my peers play is connecting the organization we are today in reality and truth to the organization we aspire to be ultimately. Managing that continuum is fraught with risk, inauthenticity, poor decision-making, and bad business decisions.

The challenge around that ethical continuum is most effectively pushing, poking and prodding organizations to fix the disconnect and to be open, honest, and transparent about that process. Many times, organizations are not even honest about there being a disconnect. We're more inclined to want to talk about our aspirational view or vision or what we desire to be in our highest and most positive light.

But we have the responsibility of not just speaking truth to power, but also doing the hard work to challenge our organizations to live up to these commitments that we most often are fine making through a very myopic marketing or PR lens. But we need to live in a broad arena.

Relationships are key. The health and import of those relationships are directly proportionate to our ability to successfully have the kinds of conversations that I was alluding to. We must do the work of building, prioritizing, maintaining, caring for and feeding those relationships at a peer level. Perhaps more significantly, we need to do this at the C-Suite level to have the types of leadership and strategic business influencing conversations that drive change.

One important caveat, there's a difference between speaking truth to power and being able to successfully influence an organization's decision-making to drive business outcomes.

Five Key Takeaways

How do we maintain the highest standards of expertise?

1. Trust your experience.
2. Confidence is contagious.
3. Offer options, not just a single solution.
4. Being an expert doesn't mean you don't ask questions or ask for help.
5. Be brutally honest in research and reporting results.

CHAPTER 5

Independence

Autonomy and independence are hallmarks of effective, ethical communicators. We are not paid to be yes men and yes women, as the PRSA's Code of Ethics highlights:

> *Independence*: We provide objective counsel to those we represent. We are accountable for our actions.

Independent Ethics Advice

Bryan Scanlon, CEO of Look Left Marketing, highlights his process for working though ethical challenges and issues to come to a decision:

There are a couple of questions that I ask myself and encourage our staff to ask every day:

- **Stop spinning.** Stop thinking about what we should say, what's the best way to say it. Take a deep breath and understand the facts without any spin. That grounds you very quickly and doesn't let you get ahead of yourself. Too often, companies instantly go into, "How do I make this better?" Or "How do I get out of it?"
- **Hit the big reset button.** Say, "I have a lot of questions about what happened, about what could happen, what we could do about it, and I'm not going to issue one recommendation on what we say or do until we understand that."
- **Ask *Why?*** Ask, "Why are we doing it? What is the purpose of this activity? What is the benefit for the company? What is the benefit for the world, society, and customers?" In other words, what problem does it solve? If you don't like the answer, you're just doing it for hype or to make somebody

happy, that'll give you an ethical barometer on which to base a decision.

Sometimes, companies go beyond inappropriate requests and make unethical requests. **Craig Sender,** Senior Director, Public and Analyst Relations, Copyright Clearing Center, highlights the three most powerful words experts use when pushing back on inappropriate requests.

Our business breeds a lot of yes men and yes women in terms of client relations. Push back on your clients. That doesn't mean be a jerk and say, "No, what are you, stupid? That's never going to work."

Push back with some strategic thought. Offer a solution, if your client says to you, "We've got a great story, we should be in the front page of the *Wall Street Journal*," I know PR people who would say, "Yes right away. We're going to work on that."

You're creating expectations that just are almost impossible to meet. In the short term, you're going to make your client happy, because they tell their boss, "My PR firm said they're going to get us in the *Wall Street Journal*." But when you don't get them in the *Journal*, you have won the battle but lost the war. You risk losing that client, and you've definitely lost their trust.

You should push back and say … and this is the key phrase, "…in my experience." That's such an important phrase because your client has hired you because you're a media expert. I don't say to my accountant at tax time, "Hey, here's how I want you to do my taxes." No, I hire my accountant because he or she is an expert in doing my taxes and I'm going to pay them money so that they're going to do it well, and it's one less thing I need to worry about.

It's the same in PR. When a client says, "We want this," it's so powerful to say, "In my experience, that might not be the best tactic right now, perhaps down the road, but let's focus on A, B and C, and then we go to D, E, and F?" And 99 times out of 100, the client will appreciate the respectful pushback.

Ethical Independence in Action

Helio Fred Garcia, President of Logos Consulting Group, discusses when and where to draw the ethical line.

The most difficult ethical challenge I faced was when my organization was dishonest. I was working full time at a public relations firm. They had a habit of lying to their clients about what they were doing. My VP told me to tell the client that we could guarantee that they would have the cover of the *New York Times Magazine*. Ethically, you cannot guarantee a result beyond your control.

And when I said, "I can guarantee I'll do everything I can to secure the cover. I can guarantee that we'll pitch the cover, but I can't guarantee that we'll get the cover story in the *New York Times Magazine*." He said, "Do it anyway." I said, "That's a violation of the Code of Ethics." The VP called me in, "So it's very clear that you have no aptitude for public relations. I don't know if you're a good fit here."

I said, "I'm certain I'm not a good fit here, and I quit." I didn't have a job to go to. But my quitting came to the attention of the headhunter who was looking for someone with integrity to represent the accounting profession.

Many years later, I was the head of communication at a big investment bank. I was hired by the CEO, and he and I had an agreement. I was the chief spokesperson for the bank. He would not lie to me. I would not lie to him, and I would not lie for the bank. He agreed to that, and we had a great relationship. Then he was fired.

A new CEO came in, he didn't agree to those terms. I naively said, "Well, I'll figure it out." I was asked to say things into the marketplace, believing them to be true. But I discovered through a *New York Times* reporter that they were lies.

I went to the CEO and said, "The *New York Times* just caught me in what I take to be a lie. I didn't intend to mislead, but you misled me. We need to have an agreement. You can't lie to me.

I can keep secrets, but you can't lie to me. I can't turn around and tell an untruth to reporters. That's going to put the bank in a lot worse shape than it is right now. And by the way, I can't sustain my career that way." He said, "Well, I'll do what I have to do as the head of the company."

A few months later, he lied to me again and asked me to turn around and tell it to the public. I verified that it was true. He affirmed that it was true. I told the news media. It turned out it was a lie too. At that point, I walked into his office, and I quit even though I was recently married with a pregnant wife. I didn't have a job to go to, and I had no idea what I would do next.

I never told any reporter about that, but by the time I got home, the phone was ringing. It was a *New York Times* guy, and he said, "Is it true that you quit instead of lying to us?" And I asked, "Is this an interview?" He said, "No, this is just us." I said, "Well, yeah. It's true." He said, "Great. You're golden. I'll trust you for the rest of your career."

Half an hour later, I got the same calls from the *Wall Street Journal* and *Businessweek.* I ended up having great relationships with those reporters who held me in good stead many years later when I had clients deep in crisis, and they needed to believe me.

When I told them what was happening, they believed me, and of course, I was telling them the truth.

The final difficult challenge was when I was at a certain PR firm, and I discovered that it was systematically cheating clients. They were double billing and billing clients for work that hadn't been done. Initially I thought it was just bad recordkeeping. I thought it was inadvertent, and I tried to fix it. But when I discovered that it was intentional and I couldn't fix it, I quit. Many of the clients ultimately discovered they had been cheated and went looking for the guy who they had trusted before. They found me, and many of them are still my clients 20 years later.

I tried to change it. In each instance, I offered alternatives, and in each instance, it became clear to me that they were determined to be dishonest. It wasn't as if they had gotten inadvertently into a bad habit. They were intentionally dishonest, and that's the line I can't cross.

There will come a point where you reach that line. I can't predict when it will be. But I can predict that you will face that line. The question is are you looking at it in the rear-view mirror or are you looking at it through the windshield. Are you approaching the line, or have you already crossed it and now you regret it?

The better you are in ethical discernment, the more likely you are to know when you are about to cross the line.

It's okay to screw up. It's not okay to be indifferent to the screwing up.

Lou Capozzi, former Chairman of MSL, highlights why you must be careful who you trust:

The most difficult ethical challenge happened to me when I was chief communications officer at Aetna.

I had a big staff, and one of the folks who worked on the staff called me at midnight on a Wednesday night and said that he had gotten a call from a local newspaper in Middletown, Connecticut, where Aetna had a remote facility with 7,000 employees. Two Aetna maintenance employees had been checked into the emergency room with chemical burns on their hands and feet, and the media wanted to know if we knew anything about it.

The answer was no, we didn't know anything about it, so I gave him the contact info for the guy in charge of the facility down there. He was told, "It was routine maintenance for the air conditioning system. Nothing to worry about." We made that statement and life went on.

The next morning, the head of that group called me and said, "You know, we've got a problem here. People have buckets on their desks and there are leaks all over the place. They've closed the salad bar in the cafeteria, because there's something dripping out of the ceiling." I thought, "Hmmmm. Two and two makes four."

I called the guy in charge of the facility, and he repeated that everything was fine. Later that morning, I get an anonymous call from somebody in Middletown, who says, "This is a bigger problem than they're letting on to you. There's mold growing in the pipes of the air conditioning system which circulate in the ceiling, and it's eating holes in the pipes."

So now I called the guy who ran the employee benefits division, and I said, I'm not getting a straight answer from your guys. Something's wrong. He called me back and said, "Everything's fine. Just a routine maintenance problem."

I had my staff dig in to determine what kind of mold. It was the mold that carries Legionnaire's disease, and it was dripping on people's desks.

I go down the hall to the CEO and say, "John, we've got a serious problem here. Your guys aren't being straight with me. There's a potential that we could have a real serious health issue with our employees. We need to shut that facility down."

It's Thursday afternoon at 4:00 and he calls the division head into his office. We sit down, and I said to them, "You've got to call the Connecticut Department of Environmental Protection. You've got to tell everybody not to come to work tomorrow. You've got to put a gate up at the entrance and send everybody home. And by the way, we'll talk about the fact that you guys lied to me another time."

The CEO turns to the division head and says, "That's what you've got to do." And so that's what happened. We sent everybody home the next day. Luckily, the environmental protection guys came over the weekend and found that it was indeed harmless, and it wasn't a risk to the health of the employees there.

One lesson I learned is to be careful who you trust, and if you don't have the CEOs support, you're in a lot of trouble. If you do have the CEOs support, then that's the magic sauce that makes this a job that can actually be done.

Kim Sample, President of the PR Council, shares her expertise in handling unethical client requests:

There are almost daily ethical questions, and most are small calls that we need to make.

Early in my career, I worked for different beer companies, and we did some things that weren't great, like a surf lifesaving competition that was sponsored by Molson Beer. That didn't make much sense.

But then, there are the outright ethical issues. I had a client a long time ago who had gotten a test opportunity in a single Home Depot store. They had to demonstrate great sales results to get into more stores. The client came to our team with the question, "What if you the agency, went and just bought our product? Made that store sell out."

I told them we couldn't do that. I went to agency leadership and had great support when I said, "We were asked to do this. This doesn't feel right. This isn't something I want our team doing." I took it to the client and said, "We can't do this, but here's how we can try to support this incredible opportunity you have in a more ethical way."

Upon hearing it, they understood immediately that what they had asked was not appropriate. Now, do I know if they got some other agency to go purchase the product? I'm not 100 percent sure. I hope not.

Sometimes, the request deals with leaking information. **Stacey Smith, APR, Fellow PRSA, Senior Counsel and Partners at Jackson, Jackson & Wagner,** shares one example:

We were working with a client who felt their organization was being targeted by a competitive organization, which had relationships with some of the local and statewide media at the highest levels. Without actual proof, but with some knowledge, this person felt that they were being targeted unfairly, even though that competitive organization was suffering from the same maladies that they were.

They came to us and said, "We want to leak something using the mail we have found out that has been bootlegged to us about that other organization. We want to send it to the media, so they see that they're doing the same things, and the coverage expands to include everybody."

We talked about it with the client and laid out that it is truly unethical to do that without any attribution. The client was pretty firm in wanting to do this. After a good hour of conversation around how unethical this is, we said, "This is not something we are willing to do, and we are urging you not to do it, but ultimately, it's your choice. If you want to share it, we at least urge you to share it up front. Put your name on it, put it out there, and let them know who it's coming from and why."

We walked away quite concerned that this was going to happen, and that we had not been successful enough in persuading this person not to do it.

I talked to them not that long after, and the person finally said, "I heard you, and I didn't do it, and we moved on." It was an interesting *in your face* ethical dilemma.

Beth Monaghan, Founder and CEO of Inkhouse, has also been asked to leak confidential documents:

The CEO of one client wanted us to leak confidential documents to the *New York Times*. These were documents that his board and other management team members did not want released. So, he thought I should do it. He gave me the package by dropping it off at my house one weekend. His rationale was that he had a confidentiality agreement with the organization. I said, "So do we."

The goal was a noble goal, which was to uncover some things that he thought were not ethical that were happening there, but the means to that goal were unethical. There were lots of discussions about who we have an obligation to and what we should do in this particular situation. I drove around with that thing in my car for two months because I didn't want anybody else to have their hands on it. At the end of the day, we decided not to do it. I said if you want to do that, it's very easy to figure out how to deliver a package to the *New York Times*, but I'm not going to do it for you. It was the right decision.

The main repercussion that you always have to consider is that you have to close your own eyes at night. It felt unethical to me as a human. We had a legal agreement with the organization. I did not have permission from the entire management team or the board to do that. I was worried about getting sued. Their parent company is a household name, and we were small business at the time. We couldn't afford to be sued by anyone.

It sounds like an easy decision, but it's not when this is a close contact of yours and he's on you to do it and you don't feel like it.

Diversity, equity, and inclusion (DEI) is one of the greatest areas of ethics focus over the past few years, and sometimes, companies want to paint a rosy picture of how they are doing. **JP Canton,** Head of Communications and Public Relations in North America for Polestar, shares an experience from earlier in his career in which he had to be accountable:

I was producing a video for internal communications and recruiting as part of my job at a wonderful company. The comms department handled all that goes into producing such a piece.

We put together our plan, and it was approved. We recruited company employees to star in the video. We found some very fun and animated folks who were very excited to volunteer and participate. We did a screen test, and grabbed a quick snippet of everyone, and their story as it related to the company. We took these rough vignettes up to HR for a review before doing a final edit. They came back and said, "Well, everything's great and it does what was promised, but we really should include a little more diversity in the video," which is a very fair point, and innocent enough at that stage.

We rounded out the gender balance and called it a day and ran it by HR for approval again. At this point, things took a bit of a turn.

HR said, "Well, hang on a moment." They pulled one of the executives into the room, who had taken an interest in the project, and the two of them proceeded to tell me, "This isn't enough diversity. We really need to include people of certain backgrounds in the shoot."

My response at the moment was, "I see where this is going, but the existing sample set of people is pretty accurate for the company. This is all starting to feel a bit uncomfortable, I understand the desire, but at the same time, this isn't quite the reality."

That's when I was given the mandate of, "Well, it's your job, you need to go recruit these specific people." I didn't like where this is headed, but I said, perhaps to my own detriment, "Let's at least go ask if these people are happy to do the video."

I popped by these folks' desks, some of whom I knew quite well. They all had no real interest and told me, "I don't really want to be on camera. It's not my thing. I'm good."

Here's where the real ethical challenge comes in because this is becoming a problem, and I had to go back to HR with it. I said, "They're not really into it." The shock was HR pushing back and saying, "You need to talk them into it because we really need them in this video, and the executive, who was in the room last time we discussed this feels the same way."

It's not an easy moment when the HR department of your employer is telling you something unethical needs to happen. That's the point where I had to fight back and say, "Look, they don't want to do it. I'm uncomfortable with the situation to begin with and you as the HR department really shouldn't be taking this track," and in nine out of 10 other companies that probably would have killed it.

They asked, "Do you want me to take this upstairs to the executive?"

Thankfully my anger kicked in and I said, "Yes, absolutely. I'd love to hear what he has to say about it."

They were kind of surprised I pushed back and said, "Well, we're going to have to have a conversation, but I'll get back to you. You're done for now."

The next morning, I received an e-mail saying, "Don't worry about it. Stick with the plan as it was." It was a happy ending, but if I had not put my neck on the line, it definitely would have gone the other way.

It made me realize that the hypothetical system of checks and balances in any well-organized company doesn't exist when somebody wants something done a certain way or to reach a certain key performance indicators (KPIs).

It was a turning point for me as a professional in which I learned it's our job as communicators, regardless of the situation and regardless of the company hierarchy, to dig in our heels and provide the right counsel. Your counsel is what you're being paid for. Doing the right thing is what you're being paid for, regardless of who or where it's coming from. It's our gut reaction as communicators to try and smooth things over or take the path of least resistance or maybe find a gray area where things work. But this is not always the best approach.

One approach I've used since, in any sort of difficult situation, is when you're speaking to somebody above your pay grade to say "I know you want this, but it's my role in the company and you are paying me to give you this counsel. I don't think your desired approach is the best end to this situation." I've found that phrasing it that way diffuses the bomb nine times out of 10. That tenth time you will have a maniacal boss who does not care and says, "I'm the boss and that's going to happen this way."

Sometimes you need say, "Put it in writing." Send that follow-up e-mail to said person and say, "You have requested me to do this. Can you please confirm this is the path you would like me to proceed on?"

In most gray areas, that will be the end of it because they understand where you're coming from and where it is going.

When it comes to duty, **Deirdre Breakenridge,** author and speaker, shares an example when two supervisors gave her conflicting orders:

There was one challenge that probably changed the way that I thought about decision-making and ethics, and it involves the truth.

As a young professional, a senior vice president gave me a specific directive. She said, "I want you to take this envelope and it needs to be hand-delivered on behalf of our client."

When I went to do it, my direct supervisor came to me and said, "Where are you going?" I explained and she told me, "No, no, no, no, no. It's okay. Everybody knows that you can just drop that in the mail."

The envelope had the address on it. The supervisor said, "Just put that in the mail because we need you here and we need you working on the event that is coming up."

I was young, I was under the impression that that was okay, and everybody knew. But I didn't know to question. I didn't go back to the senior vice president. What I did was I listened to the supervisor, I put a couple of stamps on it, and put it in the mail slot. Just as I was doing that, there was the senior vice president standing over me.

She said, "Why did you do that?" And I said, "Oh, because I thought everybody knew."

What I learned was that when somebody gives you a directive, you have to be true to yourself and true to that person. If something's going to change, you have to go back to them.

Anne Green, a Principal and Managing Director at G&S Business Communications, shares advice on how to ethically handle pressure to fudge numbers.

Very often in our field, there is a mantra that people repeat: "I'm not a numbers person." That is not a way to think. When I was building CooperKatz, we had to stamp out that language. Let's not create a self-fulfilling prophecy that we're not effective businesspeople, and that we can't learn this.

At my father's encouragement, I took the American Management Association Finance for Nonfinancial Professionals special course, just to make me comfortable at an earlier age in looking at a P&L and understanding EBITDA and other factors.

If you're feeling pressure from above to say, "These are the numbers, but let's round them up," then you can have an honest conversation.

When I was in my early 30s, senior enough as a counselor but the power dynamic was still not in my favor. I had to have the bravery to directly confront this in a thoughtful way. I said, "This can be very damaging over time if we don't have a trajectory that's backed by clarity and fact."

The other big lesson for me was it was just as important to be communicating internally about it within our agency as it was to be pushing with the client. This was an opportunity for open dialogue across all members of our account team and our leadership to say, "Let's have an open conversation about where there may be a line here and here's what I intend to do about it and here's where we're going to have to draw a line in the sand."

Some clients may say they're all rounding up. Why can't we? In some cases, it was subtle, in other cases, it got a bit more intense. In some cases, it was more about me saying, "I want to acknowledge the fact that we're making this choice to do this, and we have to be careful about how far we go."

In other cases, there were one or two times where I said, "This is just beyond the level of accuracy. From our perspective as an agency, as your agent, we are liable to the world if we're putting out information that I know is inaccurate and I'm not comfortable with that." I had to go between the different poles here of "we'll let this slide," but let us acknowledge what's happening, versus "I'm not comfortable with, period."

Katie Paine, CEO of Paine Publishing, and a Measurement Queen, has also been pressured to fudge numbers:

It happens all the time. Somebody fired us, because they didn't like our report because it didn't back up what they had to say. You just have to understand that the data is the data.

I say, "Lookie, your boss and your boss's boss and the board of directors doesn't want to make decisions based on bad data. If I do this to your data, it's going to make you look good, but it's going to lead to bad decisions."

The first thing I do is set expectations correctly and say, "I'm going to give you the data. If it's bad news, it's bad news. I'm going to give you an explanation for it and try and put it in context."

For example, I've done a lot of work for PBS over the years. They never get bad press, but every once in a while, they do. They got caught up in the Tavis Smiley and Charlie Rose #MeToo stuff. It was bad. But now we have a benchmark. Now every time there's an unusual amount of bad news, we have something to compare it to. We say, "This is bad, but it's not as bad as Tavis Smiley."

You have to get away from the win or lose mentality. Too many people look at measurement from a won/lost perspective. It's not. It's a gradual improvement process. Frankly, if you are going to get fired for speaking the truth, then you probably needed to find another job anyway.

This goes for agencies as well. I had a client where we were analyzing one announcement relative to a competitor. They didn't like the results. They said, "Well what if we just do these relevant publications?" I said, "Fine, the headline now says, 'In these relevant publications, this is how you did.'" That still wasn't good enough for them. Then they wanted me to take out a whole bunch of other stuff. I gave them the data and I said, "This data is based on four articles."

Somebody is always going to pressure you to make it look better and you just have to push back and say, "This isn't about making you look good or winning. This should be about doing better and making it better."

Independence often requires taking a stand. **Sam Villegas**, APR, a Senior Consultant with Raftelis, shares an example of when she acted as a whistleblower due to where she perceived her duties lay:

I was dealing with public outreach for infrastructure project. They wanted me to deliberately leave critical information out of the campaign materials at a time when we were looking for public support for a project. I felt like we were being misleading without sharing key information. I made a decision to share with a citizen advisory group that information, without the approval of my client. I just felt like it was the right thing to do.

When I did that, this group of stakeholders, they were so appreciative. They started immediately to troubleshoot, and to think through solutions. The city manager was willing to defer tax increases, and assessments, and the development community was going to do another thing.

The response was appropriate, and it was what you want, but when the client found out that I had revealed this information, they were very, very upset with me. I ended up resigning the client.

I did this because I've always seen my role not as a strict advocate for the client, but as a strict advocate for everybody. I walk that line between client and community and serving the public good. To my detriment, that may be too black and white for most folks. I don't see a lot of gray there, and that's on me. What we were holding back was the impact to individual rate payers. It was a material piece of information.

When you're asking for people's public support for a project, and you're leaving that out, I just felt like that was misleading. I felt that wasn't fair because if I say to you, here are all the benefits of this project. Yes, it's going to be costly, but the benefits far outweigh the costs. And I get you on board and then you find out after the fact that you've publicly said you support it, that this is a 50 to 60 percent rate increase, your mind may change. And now I've put you in this awful position of having to reverse your own public statements. I didn't want that to happen. I wanted people to have all the information, I thought that was important that they had all the information in front of them.

They ultimately called me and said, will just you come up and talk to us? We got around the table and we talked, and they said, will you tell us what this actual rate impact is? And I said, yeah. And I told them, and they said wow, that's not what we thought. That's bigger than we thought. But what can we do to mitigate it for everybody? When all the information is out, then people can roll their sleeves up and do the work that needs to be done to move forward.

I regret not being more forthcoming with the client. That's my fault. I should have gone to the client and said, I feel the need to tell the folks this. They were going to say no, but I should have told them this is my plan and let them gag me at that point. That was wrong. And that's on me. I should have told them that I was going to do it.

The other lesson, though, is that you've got to be very clear with clients from the start where you stand, what you're willing to do, and not willing to do. Another lesson I learned here is I'm not able to work for a company who sees this differently than me, who does not recognize the ethics violations. It's so shocking to me that it's more common than it is.

Sometimes your values and your organization's or client's values differ. **Ray Kotcher**, APR, Fellow PRSA, former CEO of Ketchum, provides advice on what to do:

We received a letter from the National Rifle Association. It was a very lucrative proposition. We did not pursue it. The reason that we didn't pursue it is that we had people who supported gun rights, but we had more people who did not.

I learned early on that your employees are your most important asset, and anything that is going to create dissonance and start to tear the fabric of the organization apart and create tension is something you have to think about carefully.

Early in my career, I read a book by James Autry. He was the editor of *Better Homes and Gardens*. James was a brilliant man. He eventually ended up as the president and CEO of the parent company. He wrote a book called *Love and Profit* (Autry 1992).

They were poems. They were life lessons. There were stories about critical moments that he faced.

For example, when you have to tell somebody who's been working for you for 25 years, who you know very well, and who might be your next-door neighbor and whose kids probably played with yours, that he was being let go.

How do you do something like that? What do you do when somebody who you've been working with the 25 years walks into your office and says they've been diagnosed with terminal cancer? How do you handle something like that? What I learned from him is that he thought of himself as the mayor of a small town. His decision-making was based on that idea. That he always made a decision that would be right for the common weal of the citizens of the town.

Now, did it mean that you were going to have to accept people who perhaps weren't performing at the level that they should be?

Maybe. Under certain circumstances. In any community, there are going to be people who you have an obligation to support. Society has an obligation to help people that can't help themselves. So, there may be times when you're going to have to make tough decisions like that. Are we going to extend ourselves? Are we going to help somebody because they deserve the help and they need the help? If you look at it that way and you look at it as a place where people who are contributing, people who are paying their taxes, people who are helping the growth, people who adhere to the standards in a community, those are the people who you have an obligation to protect and to support.

Taking the NRA would have started to tear the fabric of the community apart. The decision wasn't as difficult as it might be if I didn't have those guidelines as a foundation for my decision-making.

When you make these decisions, you've got to make your decisions and prove it with action. That is one of the Page Principles (Page 2022) that also are important learnings for me later on in my career. You not only got to say it, you got to do it.

Nicky McHugh, Senior Vice President, Global Content and Community at the RepTrack Company, shares an experience when she had an abusive lead and needed to speak truth to power:

> I was overseeing the corporate PR team that was one part of an even larger team in a global agency conglomerate. This group was part of a matrixed team internally that included social, branding, and advertising for a large global client. Our work was complex and challenging due to several factors outside our control. The client was being targeted publicly by a vocal activist investor, and the company was also spinning off one of its key divisions into a multibillion-dollar separate business.
>
> Internally, the lead for our agency was a person in a different division who was not managing the stress well. As a result, members of my team were working long hours and would come back from internal agency meetings in tears most days, due to the personal nature of the invective that occurred during planning sessions internally. I tried to address this management style by speaking directly with the team lead about the impact this was having. I provided tools and coping strategies to my team, and I even rotated team members so that individuals could be less exposed to this type of environment. I consulted with my boss and HR asking for help.
>
> The ethical issue is that this account was one of the top three accounts for this agency and was generating very large revenues. As such, this team lead was given large leeway in his management of the business.
>
> Nonetheless, it became apparent that the way the team lead was treating people was starting to impact all of us. Many of my teams started to manifest physical symptoms that were quite damaging, motivation issues, social issues, and after a few months, some had severe and chronic health problems.
>
> I'd escalated my requests for intervention and help using appropriate channels to my boss, our leadership team, and to HR, with no results. One day, one of my team members ended

up in hospital. That was pretty dramatic, but that's what it took to see action from the agency's leadership. Within days, my job was terminated. Within months, my boss was reassigned, the HR person left the company, and my team disbanded, many left the agency, and quite a few left the PR profession all together.

Today, quite a few years after this happened, the client is still a client with this agency, and that team lead is still managing large books of business for the agency. I remain saddened, and stunned actually, by the scope of the collateral damage, especially to the young PR folks on my team who were exposed to negative conduct, and who, in leaving the profession never had a chance to understand the power of PR, and the incredible way communications can be a force for a positive influence.

It was a big learning experience for me. It forced me to finally realize and accept how agencies operated, and it definitely impacted how I saw my world, and what I wanted as a professional.

There were a couple of key lessons from the experience.

One big lesson was, if in choosing to do the right thing, you end up challenging an institution, a legacy system, or a financial powerhouse, the odds are pretty high that you will lose. We see this playing out over and over again, most recently with the navy commander, Captain Brett Crozier, who lost his command after a letter he wrote requesting help from the navy leaders leaked to the media.

The lesson for me is that sometimes doing the right thing comes at a huge personal cost.

But the second lesson is, do the right thing anyway, especially if it aligns to your values and what you hold dear. Resilience is the best form of redemption. It's humbling how we all have the ability to pivot, to reinvent, to refocus when the universe demands it. Speaking from my personal experience, some of the best experiences of my life came about as a result of seemingly closed doors that ended up opening my eyes and my world to previously unseen and untapped opportunities.

Erica Sniad Morgenstern, Chief Marketing Officer, Virgin Pulse, shares another tough ethics challenge dealing with independence and being accountable:

> As the communicator for the organization, you always want to put out the right message. But sometimes that can be challenged by the people that you're asking to provide that message. I had a situation at one of the organizations where I worked with a very senior executive who was a spokesperson for the company.
>
> He had expertise, but when I would set him up for interviews, regardless of how much prep I did for him, he would go off the rails. He would talk about himself; he would self-promote. In some cases, that conflicted with the company messaging.
>
> I confronted him. I said, "If you cannot communicate these messages, then we're not going to use you. There are other folks in the organization that I can tap and there are other means to do this."
>
> I cut him off. For someone who is in a senior position that is full of himself, it wasn't well received. Not too much later he was let go from the organization. And he said, "You are one of the reasons why I was terminated. You did not let me fulfill a part of my job. I was supposed to be a public figure, a thought leader for the organization and you cut off my communication channel."
>
> I wasn't the sole reason, but my ethics were being attacked. I was being attacked for a judgment call I made in representing the organization. I did get some support, but I was taking sole responsibility, which isn't necessary. The organization is there to support you and I could have tapped into that some more.

Shonali Burke, Growth Strategist and Social Expert, was pressured to protect a large donor's reputation:

> I ran PR for the ASPCA for a couple of years around the time of the 2007 pet food recall. There was a lot of emphasis being put from a particular senior executive on sending out information that tried to reassure our stakeholders that a particular pet food

company was in the clear—as in their product was not contaminated—because they were a corporate sponsor.

I said, "We can't do that because we don't know that."

The concern was they're a corporate sponsor. They give us a lot of money. We need to watch out for them.

I'm like, "No, we need to watch out for our pet parents and our primary responsibility is to the animals of America."

The Web person then came to me because she was concerned with these masses of pet food that were being recalled. Every day, it was more batches being recalled. She said, "We need to do something to address these questions that we're getting."

We had already started working on FAQs that that we were sharing with everyone because pet parents around the country were calling us saying, "I don't know if my pet food is safe. Can I feed this to my dog or cat?"

So, we created the Pet Food Recall Resource Center on our website. We started to plug the batch numbers in as the FDA was releasing them to say, "This is the most up to date list of food that's been recalled. Here's what you do if your pet shows signs of illness."

In the end, that's how we addressed both our stakeholders' concerns. As our corporate sponsor did not have foods that were being recalled, we were kind of like, "Well, people can go onto the website and check if those serial numbers are there or not."

The interesting thing was that in that situation, this questionable request did not come from the sponsor, but from a very senior person inside the organization.

Dr. Felicia Blow, APR, Associate Vice President for Development and Director of Campaigns at Hampton University in Virginia, and 2022 National Chair of PRSA, shares an example when her bosses issued conflicting orders:

I was a Vice President at a Virginia community college. They had been going through an organizational transition for a years. There was shrinking enrollment, and they were trying to reach a different constituency in terms of donors.

There are 23 community colleges in Virginia, each with their own president, but there's one chancellor who oversees all of them.

The chancellor indicated he did not want media engagement around a specific issue. He had a call with all senior leaders around the state, he sent information out, and it was very clear that he was saying, "This is a party line. We will take care of this issue from the central office. Individual colleges do not need to take action. Just refer them."

So, as fate would have it, I get a call around the issue.

I went to the president, and I told him, "This is what I'll be doing about this based on the guidance we've received." At that point, he said to me, "No, this is what I'd like you to do." He put it in writing. I called and said, "Sir, just to make sure we're clear, I do not recommend we do this." I set up all the reasons and the rationale that he should have known as well as I knew, and after I sent the e-mail setting all those matters out, he picked up the phone, called me, and told me to come into his office.

When I went in, he closed the door and he repeated what he had asked me to do. He wanted my department to craft an opinion editorial on the topic that we were advised not to talk about, and to get it into the paper as soon as possible. When I came into his office, I said, "I just want to make sure we're aligned. This is the strategy I'm recommending,"

He stopped me and he said, "Let me ask you a question. Who do you report to?" I said, "You are my direct supervisor." He said, "So you do what I tell you to do." I honestly did not know what in the world to do. I was stunned. It was one of the first times I didn't have anything to say other than, "Yes sir."

What could I do? I wasn't going to quit my job or leave, but here's what I did. I called an associate in the chancellor's office and told them "I recognize and realize what the chancellor said to do, but the president has indicated that he'd like to do this, and here are the reasons he's indicated to me he wants to do it."

They told me, "Felicia, if you do this, you will be going in direct opposition of what the chancellor has asked. Don't do it."

I said, "Why don't you call the president and let him know how perilous this situation is and why he shouldn't do it?"

I went back and forth, and thankfully, a girlfriend who actually worked in a senior-level position called me, and said, "Felicia, here's my recommendation. The president is right. You do report directly to him, I would advise you to do it but the chancellor knows that he said do not do it, and your conversations with us indicating that the president has essentially threatened you is an indicator he wants you to do this badly, despite all the things that are going on."

So, I did it. He asked me to ask one of my staff persons to write the op-ed. I didn't do that. I wrote it myself. I sent it to him and asked if he wanted to issue it to the paper, and he said no and to have a staff member do it. I did it. I wanted to keep as many people out of this as possible.

Within one month of the president issuing that edict, he was fired by the chancellor. I still wrestle with that issue. It wasn't as if the president asked me to lie, cheat, or steal. He asked me to do something that was contrary to what his boss, and ultimately, my boss, if you go through the chain, said, "Don't do."

I disagreed with the state's approach, because the way the structure is set up, you don't want to have a big brother in our state capital telling all the colleges what to do. But from where I sat, I could understand why the chancellor had made that decision, and why it was taking so long for them to take action.

I guarantee you; it probably was what the president of the college was thinking too. The other side of it was truly an ego contest. He says, "I'm the president here for this college and this region." It was a contest between these two leaders.

At the end of the day, I still had to do what was right and what was right is… I don't wear my cross on my sleeve, but I'm a religious person, and one of the phrases in the Bible is obedience is better than sacrifice. That sometimes is a tough pill to swallow, but if I had to do it all over again, and a boss asked me to do something that was not illegal, immoral, wrong, and I didn't think it was right to do, unless it was something really, really egregious,

I would likely say, "Boss, I don't think we should do this, but if this is what you really want."

Here's another point. I don't work for that college anymore. I definitely don't work for that person.

It was a difficult, horrible time. I didn't want to get fired, but if I'd gotten fired for a reason like that, it would have been because of my independence.

Looking at the Bigger Picture

Despite our best efforts, sometimes we have failures of independence. **Lisa Gralnek,** Principal and Founder of LVG & Co., discusses the challenge of "me before we."

We're this tiny planet spinning in a tiny solar system in a galaxy of many galaxies. We need to come together, and so the *we* needs to lead. That attitude will hopefully impact this very near-termism approach. We need to look at the triple bottom line, meaning both profit and people and the planet.

Overcoming that shortsightedness, that near-termism, is about thinking farther ahead than next quarter's profits. We as people lack a sense of history. We have only been on this little, tiny planet that's been here since the big bang for 13.7 billion years. If you put that on a 24-hour time horizon, man has only been here for 48 seconds.

America is less than 250 years old. The Industrial Revolution, which kicked off this recent age of man, started in 1800. We're just babies, and we have to remember that. We take ourselves way too seriously. We are impatient and seek convenience. But we have to ask ourselves at some point, at what cost? I fundamentally believe that without this group collective values, we not only can't thrive, but it's questionable whether we'd survive.

Compromising your independence can often lead to lucrative short-term rewards. **Tara McDonagh,** President of Tara McDonagh Communications, discusses how do you stay true to your values and not simply chase the money:

Focus on character, not reputation. Focus on your values. If it's not hard to stand by your values, then you're doing it wrong. With the value of integrity in mind, I turned down a new business account and an agency job. Both were hard because the money would have been nice, but ultimately, it was the right decision and things fell into place.

Recently, someone I was networking with said, "Jump and the net will follow." It can be scary to turn down the money, but it's important.

Every decision I make I try to stand by what my values tell me. If I'm having a hard time making a decision, I have my core values written down to refer to. When I look at them, they can drive my decision-making, even if it's a hard decision.

Five Key Takeaways

How do we maintain the highest standards of independence?

1. We are not paid to be yes men and yes women.
2. Good leaders appreciate those who point out flaws.
3. PR professionals are the conscience of the organization. If we don't speak up, who will?
4. "It's not a big deal", or "everyone else is doing it" are specious rationalizations.
5. Always look at statements with a critical eye.

CHAPTER 6

Loyalty

Loyalty, like independence, presents some of the toughest ethical challenges for public relations professionals. The old adage: "Duty is heavier than a mountain, death is lighter than a feather" drives home throughout the ages the conflicts people faced with divided loyalties. Aside from greed, loyalty may be one of the biggest drivers of unethical behavior, for often people think they are doing the right thing, standing by a person, manager, or organization, even though the action is unethical.

The PRSA Code of Ethics states:

> *Loyalty*: We are faithful to those we represent, while honoring our obligation to serve the public interest.

Todd Van Hoosear, Chief Engagement Officer for Business Breakthrough Network, gets to the crux of the matter when he asks "What do ethical PR professionals do when they are faced with conflicting loyalties?"

For me, the toughest challenge is the big question of, to whom do you owe your allegiance? Is it your client? Is it to your agency? Is it to the media that you have to pitch? Is it to society? Who's your real boss?

For me, it has to be the media. And specifically, it has to be my reputation with the media. There were a few times when I pitched something that I didn't believe in, and it showed. It always shows. The media weren't happy. The client wasn't happy. We should have never taken the business, but we were desperate, and we did.

The great thing about ethics is it gives you a platform for making decisions that are going to be both beneficial to yourself and beneficial to society. I guess the way that I benefit myself is by not pissing off the media.

Loyalty Ethics in Action

Paula Pedene, APR, Fellow PRSA, is a PR counselor, a whistleblower, and was PRSA's PR Person of the Year in 2015. She is one of the most admirable PR people I have met, and her story of loyalty is one of the most profound of the past few decades. She goes into it in detail in her book *A Sacred Duty*,[1] but she shares a high-level overview of her story here:

I have the unfortunate, and sometimes fortunate, dubious distinction of being a whistleblower. I was backed up against a wall and had a need to share the truth, no matter how hard it was for people to accept.

We had a situation at the Phoenix Veterans Association where I was a public affairs officer for 20 years. We had some leadership changes, and we went from the "servant leader" to "what's in it for me only" leadership. Then we went from that to unethical leaders, to actually gaming the system.

I worked with another physician, Dr. Sam Foote, to expose a leader that was hurting our facility. Fortunately, we were able to share that internally with the Office of the Inspector General, and with our senior leaders above him, because they had heard some of the same rumblings and knew that something was up in Phoenix. We were able to remove him and the associate director quietly. They were left with dignity, we were left with dignity, and we went about the business of rebuilding.

Little did we know that the new leadership coming in would be worse. Except this time, those leaders knew that Dr. Foote and I had gotten rid of the former director. We had targets on our back. They figured out ways to eventually remove me from my long-standing public affairs job for a minor infraction.

I was banished to the basement for reporting violations from senior leadership. They took me out of my job, they took away my work phone, they took away my BlackBerry, they took away my VA e-mail that I had had since 1991.

---

[1] P. Pedene. 2021. *A Sacred Duty*, Skyrocket Press.

It was during this time that we found out about the worst part, which had yet to be revealed, which was the patient waits and delays, and the gaming of the system. Had I not been banished to the library, I wouldn't have heard about the additional waits and delays. I wouldn't have been able to see how they were setting up patient appointments and right before they'd hit the "submit" button to put it into the electronic system, they would hit "print." They would print the piece of paper, and then they would exit out of the computer system, and the trace of the appointment would disappear.

They had an illegal paper list supplementing the electronic wait list. The paper list kept growing. Instead of having all of the clinics working on getting those patients in, they were relegated to giving the paper to one person who was trying to make hundreds of phone calls every single day and was nearly losing her mind in the process.

When we found out what they were truly doing, that's when Dr. Foote and I just said, "We can't have it." We did what we did before, which was reporting it internally, thinking the leadership would listen. But this time, our efforts fell on deaf ears.

We worked to exposing it for a year before it finally got to the right people, and we were able to highlight what was truly happening.

Some practical advice for professionals that may encounter a similar situation.

- If you do decide to be a whistleblower, be prepared for it to take a long time, and be prepared for depression.
- You can mail something to the House Veterans Affairs Committee on Oversights and Investigations, and it gets to them. You're not transmitting from work e-mail, or personal e-mail, so you aren't violating policy.
- If you have evidence on your work computers, be sure to print it out and send it home. You want to have a backup copy and log of activities somewhere, so that if the going gets tough, you can say, "Here's what I did, here's when I

did it, and here's the evidence file." Thank God I had done that, because when they took away my e-mail, they took away my phone, they took away my office, I had no access to anything in there. Nothing. I had paper copies that I had printed and took home, that were legal for me to provide as an evidence file in reporting it to members of Congress, and to the Office of the Medical Inspector, and the Office of the Inspector General.

Karen Swim, APR, President and CEO of Words for Hire, shares an example when she was put in that difficult situation of choosing between loyalty and duty to a friend:

Prior to my PR career, I worked in the health care industry. I managed a sales team, and one of my top salespeople falsified paperwork that inflated his sales numbers. It went on for quite a bit of time undetected. When it came out, it was not only an ethical breach, but it was a breach of his employment contract, and I had to terminate his employment.

It was particularly difficult because I was a young manager who was still learning how to lead, and the person was a friend. I knew his spouse and his children. It was a stab to the heart that someone I considered to be a friend had not only committed this unethical breach, but it put me in a position where upper management was digging deep to ensure that I didn't know about it and ignored it.

I have compassion for people making bad decisions. As I matured and looked back on it, I can certainly understand that perhaps there were financial pressures that I didn't know about. However, I cemented in that moment that no matter what's going on and no matter the stress or the anxiety that you are feeling, you always have to do the right thing. The unethical behavior went undetected for a period of time, and he gained from that, but it's never okay. You are always going to win by making the right choice. Even if it costs you in the short term, it's far better to pay that cost than to say, "Well, no one's looking, I can get away with it," because the longer-term cost is far greater.

Doing the right thing is not always popular. It may cost you even when you're not in the wrong. When you're standing for ethical behaviors, not everyone will stand with you.

You need to use ethical issues as teachable moments. It was a painful time because we were a close-knit team. So, I brought them together and said as much as I could say, because at the end of the day, here was somebody who made a really bad choice, and I like to separate that out, because I don't think that he was a bad person. He made a bad choice.

I did not focus on the bad behavior, but on the situation, and how we need it to recommit to doing things the right way. I focused on creating an open environment so that if people were struggling, they had a safe forum to discuss those struggles rather than making these bad decisions.

It was an opportunity for me to reinforce the standards, for me to talk about the right and wrong things to do while also providing an avenue for people to share if they felt like they were under undue pressure, to let me be the one that removed those roadblocks, and to support them through it rather than making these difficult decisions.

Michelle Egan, APR, Fellow PRSA, Chief Communications Officer of the Alyeska Pipeline Service Company, faced an ethical dilemma when a friend asked for work after they left the company:

I was working for a nonprofit that was kind of a quasi-governmental organization, and the executive of that organization started to get a little sideways with the board.

We had an event where the mayor was upstaged a little by this executive and didn't appreciate that too much. Part of it was on me, because in my eagerness to get the mayor there (I was 30 years old at the time and pretty new at this), I didn't think he needed as much time at the event as he probably did. He ended up being tight on his schedule, and maybe even missing the opportunity to speak.

A couple of days later, the executive decided to leave the organization, and he blamed me. He told me, "If you hadn't done this thing that made this mistake that led the Mayor to lose faith, then I wouldn't have been encouraged to move on."

I knew that wasn't entirely true.

That was a little bit of an irritation for me. And it was a good thing, because a few days later when he was about to pack up to things and go, I asked, "What are your plans? What are you going to do?"

He said, "I'm going to do some consulting and I'm going to do it in this area of the organization that we were responsible for." He said, "if you want, you could work a little bit with me and help me with developing the materials that I'm going to use in this organization." I said, "Oh, that's interesting." He said, "because you know, we've developed quite a lot of material here at this non-profit, and it's aligned with what I want to do—we could just use some of that."

And I said, "Whoa, whoa, whoa, wait a minute!" I had put a lot into those materials, making them creative, attractive, and doing the research. I knew they were valuable, but I also knew that they didn't belong to me, and they certainly didn't belong to him.

I said, "That is not going to happen. Thanks for the offer, but these materials belong to this organization." And so, we parted ways.

You see that quite a bit, especially at agencies when people leave, and they ask for a media list or document they created. You need to remind them that no, it doesn't belong to you, it belongs to the client. You can use the knowledge or concepts you know, but not the materials.

Sam Villegas, APR, Raftelis, discusses *duty* and shares an example when she was asked to unethically stonewall public health issue:

There was a large national public health news story. A reporter contacted me from my local area and wanted the local angle from my client. The company was doing great things about the issue. They had a good story to tell. When the reporter called, I was pretty excited to be able to tell our angle and tell our story, that this is scary, and this is bad news, but we're doing a lot of great things about it.

When I went to corporate to share what I had planned to talk to the reporter about, they shut me down. They said, we're not going to reveal all that information. They were fearful of the media. They were fearful of what might get asked, which I am not. I welcome questions because it builds understanding, helps us get better, and builds public understanding. That's important. That's part of the job. But this corporate communications department felt differently.

They nixed my approach. The reporter was asking for some very specific numbers. So, when I wrote this very blahzy line back to the reporter, it took her about 30 seconds to respond back and say, "Are you sure you want this to be your response?" The gauntlet was thrown. If she wasn't looking for a story, now she had one. Needless to say, this saga went on for a few days over a holiday weekend.

When the reporter came back and said, are you sure you want this to be your response, I reached out to a couple of colleagues on e-mail because I had a stomachache, and I said, listen, here's the situation. My gut is telling me I've got to remove myself, because I feel my company is asking me to stonewall, and it doesn't feel right. It's not in the interest of the public. It's not in the interest of the company. God love my network, because they came back and they said, yeah, your instincts are right.

I went back to corporate, and I said, listen, I'm removing myself from this conversation. I could do that because I wasn't an employee, I was a consultant. I thought, well, they could fire me, but for my own reputation with this reporter, I'm not going to go through with this sham. Corporate said fine, have her reach out to us. She did, and they stonewalled her. About a week into it, they finally gave her the information that she wanted, but it was a little too little too late.

The tragedy is the company had a good story to tell. They were just afraid to tell it.

Mark Mohammadpour, founder of Chasing the Sun Health Coaching, also discusses what do you do when your work does not align with your personal values:

One of the proudest pieces of business I had the opportunity to work on was the U.S. Army. In 2009, the United States was in multiple wars in Iraq and Afghanistan, while domestically we were in a recession. There was a definite need to bring more soldiers into the Army to serve. This was before Twitter was big, this was before Facebook for brands, there was no Instagram. But there were more prospects coming online to learn about what Army life was like. Unfortunately, at that time, the Army wasn't in those conversations, and there was a need to build out its digital assets and conversation opportunities for prospective soldiers to learn about what the Army was like. A lot of that was already in motion at Weber Shandwick, but I was brought in and added to a growing team to help tell the story of the Army soldier.

When I was asked to join the team, there was this question in the back of my head, as far as, "Okay, we're in a war, is the war the right thing that we're doing right now?" I had to weigh that with what was really the ask, to tell the story of the Army soldier. The Army was very supportive and understanding that it had to be very transparent. They needed soldiers to blog and to share stories and be very transparent about what life is like in the Army, the good or the bad. As long as it didn't violate operational security, the Army supported these soldiers writing blogs and having videos taken of them that were run by our team.

This made me feel a lot better about joining this account, because there definitely was in the back of my head, "My God, I don't necessarily believe that we should be in a war right now." But to help support the soldier and their story and to give people who are interested in joining the Army as much information as possible so that they could make an informed decision was fine.

If people find themselves in similar situations, they need to realize that you can say no. That is a scary thought to have. We're people pleasers, we're in the service industry. We're used to solving problems. It's empowering, especially in today's era to be able to say, "This does not align with what I'm doing." But at the same time, you need to be prepared to say why.

Chris Penn, Cofounder and Chief Data Scientist for Trust Insights, shares what he did to help him sleep at night when he realized his personal ethics conflicted with his company's ethics.

I worked at a company that fundamentally created and resold student loans. Our job was to put people in debt.

Banks and lending companies paid thousands of dollars per loan application, particularly for federal student loans, because they were guaranteed by the government. They were super low-risk financial contracts that they could then blend into higher-risk contracts and create these things that eventually led up to the 2008 recession.

The personal challenge was we were fundamentally making the world a worse place. Yes, people are getting access to education, but at an extremely high cost. They may not be able to pay it back. So, the challenge was, how do we balance the business need with the human need?

I went the route of creating content for free. I created The Financial Aid Podcast in 2005. I did 934 episodes of that, 15 minutes a day, every weekday, for five years.

I created seven editions of a scholarship search eBook, which is still mostly relevant today. My ethical balance was I have given you five years of daily information, and seven books on how you can go to college for free. It requires a lot of work to apply for scholarships. Treat it like a full-time job.

If you don't want to do that work, then here's a loan application. Now, you understand the tradeoff. You can put in the hard work now and not have to pay back the money, or you can take the easy path and then end up having to pay the money. But at least, ethically, I gave people the choice.

Dr. Felicia Blow, APR, Associate Vice President for Development and Director of Campaigns at Hampton University in Virginia, shared how her loyalty was tested when her employer lied to her:

> When I was a public affairs specialist, many years ago, I was on camera weekly because we were a high-profile organization, and what we did was of interest both to the media and the citizenry.
>
> There were at least two separate examples where senior leadership misinformed me about a matter. I went on camera, reported one thing, only to have to do a mea culpa the next week when it was discovered that what I indicated was not true.
>
> The last time it happened, it was damaging to my personal reputation. So much so that I debated leaving. I called the board chairman and said, "I refuse to do this anymore. I am not going on camera to talk about X." I got personal assurances from the executive director that I would never be put in those circumstances again. I never trusted certain folks in certain departments, ever again, and I would qualify every answer, stating, "As you can see in our annual report, it is noted X, Y, and Z. Should this change, I will follow up."
>
> But with some of the reporters, my credibility never was restored.

Loyalty, Racism, and Sexism

While there has been significant progress in the industry on issues of racism and sexism over the past few years, there is still a long way to go. **Cedric F. Brown**, APR, an independent consultant, discusses your duty when you see racist behavior at work.

> I had to confront racism at work. I noticed that some Black colleagues of mine were sharing a lot of the same experiences that they were having with particular staff members and particular members of senior leadership. It was to the point where some of my colleagues would be in tears because they were berated over their work, among other pretty blatant actions that were taken

against them. These actions and the way they were treated drove some of my colleagues away from the organization.

It felt like at times, our senior leaders just sat on their hands and did nothing about the problem for people of color in the organization. When I had the opportunity, I spoke up. I couldn't bottle in the frustration that I had felt, especially when one colleague of mine was a mid-level professional, who had spent several years in the organization, moved on based on the way she was treated. She deserved better. That's all I want for Black and Brown professionals, diverse professionals, regardless of your race, your age, your orientation, your religious beliefs. Everybody should be treated fairly.

I was at this particular organization long enough where I felt comfortable that I was providing enough value in my actual work to speak up because I could risk being targeted for retaliation. I strongly believed the quality of my work would make it tough to get rid of me. What I would advise others, unfortunately, is to be able to play corporate games a little bit. Demonstrate that you bring so much value to the organization that you make it hard for people to part ways with you.

With the issues of racism in the workplace, many people carry out microaggressions. Things that on the surface, come off as compliments, but are not. They might be unintentional; they usually are unintentional. If you as a white man, comment on me being articulate, that's microaggression because it's steeped in this idea that I probably wouldn't speak properly because of the way I look. There are other microaggressions Black women will often face and hear such as, "I like how you wear your hair a certain way, usually straight and 'neat.'" That's based on your Eurocentric standards, and honestly, our standards of professionalism in the workplace and in corporate America are defined by old white men. We have to reimagine what we consider *professional.*

When you're looking to talk about racism and address issues of race in the workplace, the advice that I give is to never call out specific people. As you can see, I'm doing my best to not disclose the names and their identities. You have to be able to pinpoint that it's not one specific person (if it's not one specific person) but paint it as it being a trend.

Angela Sinickas, CEO of Sinickas Communications, gives another perspective on what to do ethically when you realize you work at a company rife with sexism and racism:

I didn't realize that it was an ethical challenge right at the beginning, but it became more of a challenge for me to get myself up in the mornings and go to work. I had been working at a consulting firm for about six years, and I was on track to be invited to become a partner. But I was becoming more and more uncomfortable working there for a number of reasons—mostly due to racism and sexism.

I remember in the hallway outside of our communication consulting area, there was a very senior partner in our office talking to another very senior partner who was my boss, and it was Christmas time. We had a Toys for Tots drive going on. We all brought in unwrapped presents to put under the tree, and these guys were talking about the black Ken doll that was under the tree and making totally inappropriate comments about black men. As heinous as that was, they were also having this conversation right in front of the office of one of my colleagues who was not Black, but her husband is Black. They saw no problem with having these kinds of conversations and laughing in public. You can't change how a person is deluded and sees the world, but you should be able to control what they expose other people to in the workplace.

Sexism was very similar. Very few women were invited to become partner and primarily only if they didn't have children. There were a whole series of things going on, and so I had begun raising my voice to say this isn't right.

I didn't call that partner out. I certainly was not in a position to do that, but talking with my own boss, talking with HR, and the result of that was they still wanted me to stay on the partner track, but they put me through counseling because they thought the problem wasn't the firm or the partners, they saw the problem as me. The counseling they put me was to teach me how to do only what was my job to do and not to worry about the things that were not mine to do.

That solidified it for me. They thought that they weren't acting inappropriately. They thought I was acting inappropriately by calling them on it. That's when I decided I needed to leave. I gave my announcement, and the CEO of the company flew in from headquarters to try to talk me out because I was doing a good job for them. I was bringing in revenue. I explained to him that I couldn't stay for all these reasons. He said, "Yes, but we can change." I said, "You might be able to, but it's going to be a long, long time."

The problem with being a partner in the organization was it went beyond just being an employee. These people also spend time outside of the office together. They'd buy their vacation homes in the same places. I could not see myself living in that world with those people even beyond work. It was a simple decision when I finally came to it. The problem was, I walked away from a lot of money because those people not only made a lot of money, but they eventually sold their firm and they all cleaned up huge. Do I have any regrets? Yeah, I wish I had the money. But do I have any regrets about my decision? Absolutely not.

My advice for others is you've got to decide what is the end result that you're looking for. Because if you do want to stay there, then you have to go to extraordinary lengths to try to change the place. If I'd had more confidence in myself (I was only in my early 30s at that point, probably didn't get that kind confidence until I was 40), I probably would have gone into the office of those different people one on one and just said something more like, "I don't know if you realize this, but I have a problem. My problem is when I hear these things being said, I feel this way."

I can't change the way you feel about things, but please don't do that in the workforce around me. That's just a human-to-human conversation. It's not a junior person to a senior person. It's just saying this makes me very uncomfortable. And I'd rather, if you had these conversations, you didn't do it in my presence. Speak out, but say it one on one in a private setting and explain why it's a problem for you personally rather than just pointing fingers at them—because then they don't listen.

Too often we keep quiet for too long, and that makes it harder to speak up. **Mark Cautela**, Head of Communications for Harvard Business School, shares his opinion on why you need to act quickly and decisively on even small ethics concerns:

I was a junior person in a room, and a more senior person started to use off-color language that today, with both the #MeToo movement and the Black Lives Matter movement, would be cause for dismissal. But at the time, it was sort of an old boys' club network type of thing where that was more accepted. I felt uncomfortable at the time. Things were said in the presence of women and minorities that I didn't feel right about.

I didn't stand up and say anything at the time. And that one eats at me. Should I have said something? Should I have done something there? Should I report that person?

In some cases, the comments were made when it was just me and this person. By not doing something very early in the relationship, it set the standard that they thought it was okay for them to talk and behave like that around me. It created a challenge for me with working with this person.

I had to ask myself what are you going to stand up for? What are you going to believe? If that person were to say that in front of your friend that was a minority or a woman, what would you do in that case? Would you let them do that right in front of your friend? And if you wouldn't want them to do it then, why is it okay for them to do it when they're not around? Is this the kind of person you want to work for, or the kind of company you want to work for that allows that to happen?

I thought of that again as these things were unfolding over the last couple of years. I thought of myself in that situation. Yes, it was a different time back then, but I still knew better. I was always wondering why I didn't say something sooner or why I didn't make a change. In the end, that person was called out for that very thing, and eventually let go, but it wasn't until several years after I worked with them.

It is something I think about a lot, and it never left me feeling well about the way I handled it. One thing I would've done differently, I would have established early on with that relationship that kind of talk wasn't going to be okay with me, and let that person know that I would be willing to go to HR if it didn't change. Once that precedent is set, you enter this dark spiral where it gets worse and worse.

This is the case with many ethical challenges that people face. No one ever starts out by saying, "I'm going to defraud the company of millions" or, "I'm going to create a toxic culture." It starts with little things. It's one number is fudged or it's one comment made, and it goes unchecked, and so the person feels emboldened to make another comment, or they feel okay to maybe fudge more numbers, or maybe add a penny here or a dollar there, or a plus versus a minus, and it all adds up eventually.

Keeping quiet can create and enable a toxic culture. It's not necessarily one person. It's usually a culture. Culture is created by the way we handle our business on a day-to-day basis. If we are unethical or if we let things slide that we know we should correct, those add up, and the people that work in that company, that don't stand for those things, they notice. Today, with the way social media has emboldened people to have a voice and to speak up, your company, your institution, your culture is much more likely to be called out for something like that.

It's up to you as a leader to make those hard calls and take the decisive action to stop that as soon as you hear it. It is easier said than done, but luckily, I've had the opportunity in my career to also work for some great people that I admire a lot who were strong leaders, who had that voice, and would do what they thought was right. If you can surround yourself with those people and work for those companies, you're going to find yourself feeling a lot better about yourself personally, and not just your career.

Loyalty Ethics Advice

Karen Swim, APR, President and CEO of Words for Hire, believes ethics trump any agenda:

So often, the ethical issues that are brought to the public's attention send a message that an agenda is more important than ethics. Ethics decisions are made through the lens of the results. You have companies and the government that act in unethical ways, but they get a pass if the results are there. They only don't get a pass when the results fall apart.

As PR people, we are the guardian of ethics. We have a duty to ensure that it is enforced. We have a duty to protect the clients, the organizations that we work with, as well as the publics that we serve. But when we are working in an environment where it's seen that ethics doesn't matter, if you're getting the results over here, then we'll just sweep this under the rug, that is dangerous.

We have to have a louder voice. We have to educate, we have to advocate, we have to guide. In my opinion, having an ethical framework is not just a nice thing to have, it drives profitability.

Trust is critical to a company's survival. If the public doesn't trust you, then they're not going to buy from you. When there's trust internally, you have employees who are advocates for your organization, you have more cooperation, you have higher productivity, that results in happier external customers, and it means that they're going to make the right decisions.

Our role is to draw the lines for corporations and to be the voices that are louder than people saying, "Ethics is not so important." We have to take a harder stance and speak up. Professionals must speak in a language that is meaningful to an organization. If you just talk about ethics, it could fall on deaf ears, but when you translate it into language that they understand, then you can definitely move the needle and have influence.

Sometimes, your boss asks you to burn bridges as **Sherry Feldberg,** Principal, Leadership Journey, recounts:

I was leading a response to a crisis communication situation where a client had a pretty unfavorable story come out. I fundamentally disagreed with the strategy my manager wanted to push forward. It was tied to letting the reporter know how angry and disappointed we were on the way the story came out.

There were no inaccuracies in the story, there was no false information to ask for a correction. It was really just to express that sentiment. It felt very wrong and not in line with my values. I'm all about building relationships with people.

It bothered me too that in trying to explain some of my rationale and have a conversation about it, there was no desire from my manager to understand a different point of view. Then to make it even worse, I had a colleague who was privy to the situation, essentially say, "Well, why don't you just say you'll do it and then don't do it."

I was like, "What? I can't do that." That's just so dishonest and not the way that I want to carry myself professionally. I wouldn't feel okay about that and hearing that from a colleague was like pouring salt on the wound.

If others find themselves in a similar conversation, my best advice is we can make any point we want to make. It's the words we use and the way we position things. Do not be highly emotional about it. Stay calm and make it clear that you'd like to have a conversation. Start by asking to have more of an open dialogue so that you can better understand their point of view. Then ask for the opportunity to express your thoughts as they stand now and just see if we can see each other's points of view and see if perhaps that changes anything in the situation.

Approach it calmly. Don't say "I can't believe you'd asked me to do this." Don't be accusatory or use a lot of the "you, you, you." It's when people either are too afraid to say something, so they don't say anything, they feel like they have no choice, or they just use a lot of emotion, is when it goes south quickly.

Dr. Joe Trahan, APR, Fellow PRSA, a 30+-year PR pro, and retired Lt. Col in the Army, shares advice on where your loyalty lays with your boss:

I was two doors from the boss, and one of the things I said when I interviewed with him, was I wanted direct access to him. He wasn't too happy with it initially. I told him, sir, I'm going to tell you when it's bad and when you're ugly. When I tell you that, I'm going to also offer you solutions.

In all my career, I've never purposely lied in a news conference. I've been truthful and said I don't know something. We have a responsibility to advise our clients, our bosses, and say, this is what's happening, and that's what I would do.

The Army taught me, problem, discussion, recommendation. I would identify the problem, I would come in and discuss, and then I offer solutions.

You have to be the voice. You have to speak up, I've been shut down numerous times. I've been told to shut up. I remember generals chewing me out—Trahan, all you do is bring me grief. I said, yes sir, but I'll bring you solutions.

I remember a general telling me, you always want me to do the right thing. Yes sir. We'll never go wrong. Even if we make a mistake doing the right thing. Our job is to be vigilant. Our job is to represent our organization. However, if our organization is doing things that are wrong or unethical, we need to take it first internally.

I've had some other friends when I went through this years ago say, well, why don't you take that to the media? I felt a responsibility to my organization first. I was Don Quixote, charging windmills. You go in there and you say, this is the problem I see, this is the discussion, here's the three courses of possible action, and I recommend this course of action. That's where we earn our keep. That's where we make sure we're sitting next to the boss like the lawyer is.

In all the interviews I have done on ethics, this advice from **Michael Smart,** a leading media relations trainer and coach, is the one I come back to most often and tell others:

This advice was given to me by Dr. Laurie Wilson, one of my PR professors at Brigham Young University. As we were getting closer to graduation, we were doing a real raw Q&A with her, and one of us asked "What do you do if you're in a position and your employer asks you to do something inconsistent with your values?" She said, "Start right now saving your freedom fund." She recommended we save three months' salary so that when you're put in that position, there may be other reasons you might consider how to comply with what your boss wanted you to do, but if it was a violation of your ethics, you wouldn't cave because you needed to eat or pay the rent.

I took that to heart. I saved that freedom fund. It was even more relevant to me, because my wife and I had our first child when we were 25, and we always saved so that we didn't have to make that kind of decision. When I started my business, I made sure I had enough saved so I wouldn't have to take or keep a client that would put me in a difficult situation.

Five Key Takeaways

How do we maintain the highest standards of loyalty?

1. Determine where your true loyalties lay.
2. Loyalty is not the same thing as blind obedience.
3. Loyalty is a two-way street.
4. Don't cut and run the first time you see a problem.
5. As Michael Smart says, build a freedom fund.

CHAPTER 7

Fairness

Fairness is an interesting topic. Today, fairness is being downplayed compared to equity, but it is still relevant and essential.

The PRSA Code of Ethics states:

> *Fairness*: We deal fairly with clients, employers, competitors, peers, vendors, the media, and the general public. We respect all opinions and support the right of free expression.

Fairness Ethics in Action

Layoffs

Fairness is questioned more often during layoffs, promotions, and hiring than anywhere else. The following examples get to the heart of the matter.

Layoffs are a fact of life in corporate America. **Anthony D'Angelo**, APR, Fellow PRSA, Professor at the S.I. Newhouse School at Syracuse University, discusses how to handle them ethically and fairly:

The most difficult ethical challenge I've encountered goes to the number of gut-wrenching reorganizations and layoffs I've had to announce as a director of communications in the corporate sector. I have announced no fewer than a dozen plant closings. I was the person interviewed on the evening news talking about the bad news that was going to strike a community and the residents of it.

These things are never easy. At some point, I found myself questioning my own ethical stance in terms of what was right— for the company that I was working for was actually doing very well financially.

I had personal relationships with many people who lost their jobs. I asked myself, what is right here? These people are every bit as good at their positions as I am in mine. They are losing their jobs, and I'm starting to struggle with it.

The conclusion that I came to was that I had to look at it on behalf of the long-term success and vitality of the organization to survive and thrive in a hyper-competitive environment. Sometimes that entails very, very difficult decisions. We needed to make decisions based on the long-term health of the company, and that had to do with taking responsibility for the employees that work for us, the shareholders that owned us, and the communities where we operated, so that the company could fulfill its role in society.

We also had to take a long view so that we would treat everyone in a way that went well beyond simply cutting them loose. I was very pleased the company took extraordinary measures to offer them other employment opportunities within the company, to extend severance and health benefits and to extend education benefits for retraining.

Ethics is not a transactional decision that you make once, it's a way of life that you conduct over a marathon in the life of an organization and the life of the people who populate it.

A major portion of working through wrenching change is to answer the *why* questions and not just the *what*. Too many times, companies making these sorts of announcements simply say what is happening. We are having a 15 percent workforce reduction, here is your severance package. Thank you very much.

That is fundamentally unsatisfying to people because nature abhors a vacuum. That kind of simple presentation of the ultimate decision, treated as though it is the complete communications will usually lead to a very difficult and controversial road ahead.

Compare that to answering the why. For the company that I was working for, the why had to do with unbelievable price competition from China, long supply routes, and the lack of plant expansion ability.

In these sorts of situations, it is at least as important for our public relations professionals to bring the outside environment in. It becomes an educational venture, so the people understand the factors that we're dealing with. Too many times, we treat it as we need to get our story out, but a free flow of information into the organization will turn the conversation in the right direction. It won't be easy, but you have a shot at making it more effective.

It works. I remember one employee was interviewed by the media at a plant gate the very day that I announced a plant closing. The employee said, "I don't like the decision that was made today because of the effects on me, but I understand it. I see the rationale, and understood the company had to make decisions."

In a difficult situation, that's about the best you can hope for.

Our chief legal counsel once told me that it is his job to tell me the legal considerations, and that all decisions carry a degree of risk. Based on that, it's up to all of us to determine what's our risk tolerance based on all the factors that need to go into the discussion. That was very helpful and instructive for me because here was an attorney taking a broader view of the entire organization and understanding his responsibilities.

That encouraged me to take a broader view of the entire organization and my responsibilities as a communications professional. I had to be as willing to listen as I was to talk. That goes for everybody around the table in those kinds of situations.

The key lesson is to have an ethical stance and know what you're about. I believe wholeheartedly that your foundation has to be a Code of Ethics. It's important to know what you stand for and know what your organization stands for so that you can ask yourself, what's the end game here? What are we truly trying to do in the midst of a very trying time, for there will be other trying times.

It's important that we behave in the direction of the values that we've said we've signed up for. I have found that that's served organizations well and it also serves people well.

Mike McDougall, APR, Fellow PRSA, President of McDougall Communications, also had ethical issues with plant closings:

During my time in-house, we were going through a series of changes in the organizational structure. One of those changes meant closing a sizable manufacturing facility overseas. That's not atypical in today's environment, but the ethical challenge was on a few fronts.

One, we had just been to that facility a few months prior with a new CEO, talking to that employee base on how valued they were, how incredibly important they were to the organization and the future of the organization. Now, six months later, we found ourselves facing the need, because of production capacity issues, to shutter that plant. You had an ethical issue of what did we tell you. Was it the truth? Was it not? How does that square with what we're about to do?

The second ethical issue was community-facing. Could you go in and essentially create a significant hole in the community where that facility was located? We were the fifth largest employer in a large metropolitan area in the UK. There would be consequences to that community.

The third ethical issue were some guarantees that we had made to government about labor and about staffing levels. Here's the unique thing. By the time we would announce the plant closing, we would have met those guarantees for staffing and could essentially retain a significant amount of investment made by local and the federal government. However, would it be ethical to do so? Should we retain those funds? Technically, we had earned them, but quite honestly, three or four days outside of the window where we earned them, we're announcing we're shutting the plant down.

In this situation, we advised our CEO to do a couple of things. One, we need to go in and tell the truth. We need to explain that at the time, they were extremely valuable. They still are, but in weighing what the future of the organization looked like, as a whole, we needed to take this action. By not doing so, we were putting the entire organization in jeopardy. As much as this is news, we didn't want to have to bring to them, it was incumbent that we do so.

The second thing, and he agreed to it, is he needed to deliver the messages. Do not pawn this off to somebody else to go in and clean it up. That's the mark of a leader. He was very willing to do so. That helped us and won the respect of the other plants as well.

I remember vividly standing with him here, and outside a meeting where we were discussing what we needed to do I said, "In my view we need to go back in person. You need to go on to the plant floor and address not only one shift but all three shifts of employees. Tell them this to their face."

He said, "That's the right thing to do. I'm not going to like it. It's not going to be fun, but it's the right thing to do, so let's make it happen." But there are other considerations that come with that. As a multinational with some prominence, there's some risk. We not only had him prepared from a messaging standpoint, but we prepared him from an emotional standpoint.

We did some training with him with other members of our executive team at the time. We had some of our team mimicking what we thought we'd see, truly lashing out, blaming these executives not as a company but personally for ruining their lives, creating issues where kids might not be able to return to college, questioning if they can put food on the table.

We kept our commitment to the community as well. As a communications team, we convinced the organization to hand back the investment that had been made in whole to the UK government and say we don't need to, but this is the right thing to do. We cannot walk away from this in good faith taking your money and closing the plant.

The money involved was considerable. It was material in terms of the amount of cash that would be returned. There were certainly voices in opposition to that from purely a financial perspective, but we couched it by saying by doing this we expect to achieve a better return than we otherwise would. Ultimately, the government, on the floor of the parliament, said this is one of the best corporate closures of a site they had ever seen. Which was certainly a nice compliment. I wish it was a compliment that never had to be made, but the thought was, "You did it the right way."

A few key pieces of advice:

1. Don't overpromise.
2. What you do promise, make sure you can fulfill.
3. Make sure that the services you're putting in place are not just for show. They're actually going to help those who are affected. We asked local community leaders and the local HR teams what skills were most needed in that community? What skill sets could be transferable from the employees who would be displaced? We set up job training programs specific to the needs of that community, as opposed to just a generic job skills program that we could have put anywhere in the world.

Did it completely mitigate us leaving? Absolutely not. Did it help? Yes. You want to make sure you're being seen as helpful as opposed to just checking the box and moving on.

One ethical point often overlooked with layoffs is balancing the ethics of communications with those employees laid off with those employees remaining to avoid a second exodus or minimize negative reaction according to **Anthony D'Angelo**, APR, Fellow PRSA:

Too many times, the survivors are neglected in the communications plan. Ethically, that should never happen. Part of the education process has to be with the employee base. They will certainly be disturbed by news of a facility closure or a major layoff. They need to know the way forward.

Companies need to take a look at the long term and decide what they need to have for a healthy organization. That means your customer comes second. In other words, your employees come first because the way they are treated and the way that they see fellow employees treated, including those who may be losing their jobs, will have a great deal to do with their outlook on the company and their work ethic going forward.

I can't emphasize enough how difficult this work can be. I often ask my students: how would you feel if you had a number of friends that were working in a facility that you knew was being planned to be shuttered in six months? Do you feel okay keeping that confidential? Because you have to keep confidential, make no mistake about that.

That usually leads to a very spirited classroom discussion that goes to the idea that a public relations professional has to operate honorably and transparently. At the same time, however, we are unabashed advocates for the organizations that we counsel. One of the principles of the Code of Ethics is to safeguard the confidences of our employers.

So, we are beholden to that because we are there to advance the interests of the organization.

Elizabeth Pecsi, APR, Fellow PRSA, former Director of Executive Communications, Unisys, has also dealt with the issue from a media relations perspective.

I was working with the media when I was at a large publicly owned utility. They were making some changes in the way that it was going to run the utility.

I had quite a number of good relationships with the media, and some of them asked, "Why don't you tell me about this? I understand that there are some changes going to be made in terms of how you're going to be running the business."

I realized I had to be very careful here. We were a publicly held company. This particular reporter kept poking me, saying, "Hey, you're my buddy, can't you give me some insight on this?" And I was like, "No, I really can't." It was a very awkward situation because I was friends with this person before the situation came up. But I realized that the risk and responsibility outweighed doing something for a friend.

Fairness to Employees, Clients, and Society

Part of fairness is fighting unconscious bias. We all have it, and **Mickey Nall**, APR, Fellow PRSA, and past Chair of PRSA, discusses how to avoid it:

We had a chief diversity officer who was challenged in the United States to come up with a training program to help recognize bias, and how to navigate through that. This training was mandatory, for all levels. No exceptions. No "I'm senior, I'm so important, I've got client meetings." Training gives you the necessary tools to navigate these minefields to make the situations better.

You would sit in the room with your colleagues, and you would go, wow I'm hearing stuff out of his mouth that is totally not acceptable. They're not meaning to be unacceptable. They just either didn't know better or didn't care. You can't train people to care but you can train people that these are the guard rails that they need to stay between. That helped a great deal on the diversity side of the equation pretty quickly. What we did not do well on was inclusion and retention. We were constantly hiring great people, and yet they weren't staying.

The key, to me, of inclusion, is it's one thing to invite everyone to the party. We'd invited everyone to the party, look at the party, it's so optically perfect now. But you know what? Until somebody walks across that room and invites that person to dance at the party it's not inclusive.

We needed to take a step back. We had invited people to the party, but we weren't asking anybody to dance. So, we formed some communities around likeness. We had a Latina community, we had an LGTBQ community, we had an African American community, we formed communities in each office so that people could support one another. And we had to put the resources behind it. We found if there is a community within the company you can go to with your issues and problems first, there will be someone in that community, stronger, more senior, more experienced, that can then go to management and say here's an issue that we can fix.

For example, one group of creatives had a wonderful, ongoing happy hour session, where they played golf at a driving range. But several people in that group felt that it had become very cliqueish, and they didn't like that. But nobody wanted to say anything, because they work in that department, they didn't want to get into trouble or to be ostracized.

Once that was brought to my attention through one of the communities, I could go sit with the head of that department and say, "Here's the issue, we either need to revamp that or I'm going to need us to do something different." This executive was mortified. He was fighting for budget to keep doing this, and it was actually working against his team. He stopped and did something else. That increased our retention.

Being fair to employees, means dealing swiftly with high-performing, toxic employees according to **Beth Monaghan,** founder and CEO of Inkhouse:

Conventional wisdom is that one negative person in the office can ruin the entire office culture. That is something every leader knows. You should coach them or fire them if that's not possible as soon as you possibly can. Where this becomes tricky is when that person is also one of your top performers. Perhaps they bring in a lot of business, perhaps you'll lose clients. You are forced to choose between immediate financial ramifications and the people who work with that person all day long. Sometimes, that can be a very hard decision because every business has very real bottom line issues to attend to.

For me, we get rid of that person, and we've done it more than once. It's always been the right decision. Always. Even in a few times where I thought, wow, this person might have a bunch of people fooled, I've come in the next day and the entire atmosphere in the office has shifted.

It's hard to make those decisions but if you choose what is right for your people, the rest will follow. It's kind of like a karma situation where you have to hope that if you do the right thing, the right thing will follow you around. I believe that to be true.

Fairness to clients is another key issue, and one unethical element too many firms do is the insidious practice of double billing. **Adam Ritchie,** Principal of Adam Ritchie Brand Directions, explains:

At one point in my life, I was on a team that while you were traveling for one client you were encouraged to do work for other clients and bill the same hour to two different accounts. This is the practice that I think a lot of agencies do called "value billing." And I always thought, yeah, that's valuable to the agency, but is it valuable to the client?

On the flip side of this, I once had a client of my own tell me that I was acting unethically because I always bill for travel time. I'm always transparent about that, and I build it into every project that requires it.

She said, "We don't pay people while they're sleeping on a plane." I actually had to argue that I can't sleep on planes, and I spend that travel time working on that account. What I wanted to say was, I'm sure when you're sleeping on a plane, you're getting paid for it because you get a regular paycheck from a company. And I don't, that's what you want to say. But you have to say the other thing.

Sometimes, writing off costs is a component of fairness according to **Martin Waxman**, APR:

When I decided to invest time in the P&G campaign, we had to scrap due to 9/11, I spoke to the CEO, and he was very open to it. He was all about relationships. He came from a political background, so he knew the value of long-term relationships and what you needed to do to maintain them. It's not, "We do it, we bill you, next." It's not transactional.

If you are just transactional, it's easy for a client to walk away. But if they feel their agency is not only invested but has their best interests at heart, even when it impacts the agency's bottom line, the client starts to believe and trust you more and think, "Yeah, these people are looking out for me," and they'll have a conversation that maybe they don't want to have because it's the right thing to do.

This applies to clients as well. Early on, we fired our largest client when we only had eight clients. That was a huge decision. But our team valued that, and they became a lot more loyal because they knew that we had their backs. You just can't put up with people being abusive to your staff; otherwise, you won't have a staff.

Jim Olson, former Global Corporate Communications lead for Starbucks and U.S. Airways, shared insight from his time at Starbucks as they grappled with a number of ethics issues around fairness:

One of the higher-profile situations that I had to contend with was after the Sandy Hook Elementary School shooting in Connecticut, where 20 children and six adults lost their lives. One of those teachers, Lauren Rousseau, was a part-time barista at Starbucks. Guns and gun violence have always been a politically and emotionally polarizing issue for the United States. This time, it was one of our own that had been directly affected by it. We as an organization, our team at Starbucks, where I was serving as the head of global corporate communications, were actually, for the first time in my life and as an organization, directly connected to this issue.

In the weeks that followed the Sandy Hook shooting, many of our stores became a battleground for the gun debate. On the one hand, you had very vocal gun violence advocates, legislation advocates, fighting for more legislation. On the other side, you had very strong, vocal Second Amendment advocates.

What we found was a very visible presence of firearms, and sometimes very large firearms, showing up in our stores. Thankfully, there was no violence associated with those, but for many of our employees and for many of our customers, it was counter to the warm and welcoming atmosphere that we tried to create. We were essentially faced with almost an impossible choice to make as an organization. We either were going to have to ban guns from our store and essentially provoke a Constitutional firestorm or continue to comply with states' open carry laws, which is what we had been doing previously, and jeopardize that warm and welcoming family atmosphere.

We had thousands of stores across the country, spanning red states, blue states and purple states. Our employees, customers and investors were passionately on both sides of this issue. Essentially, we thought in our minds, it was going to be a no-win choice. We debated it for weeks or even a couple months. We had some very lively and passionate debates and very intellectually honest debates within our organization, all the way up to Howard Schultz, our chairman and CEO, and the board. But what makes this story a great learning lesson is that we ultimately landed on neither of those choices.

Instead, we took out full page newspaper ads and utilized our social media channels to deliver an open letter from our chairman and CEO, Howard Schultz, to the country, respectfully requesting that gun owners not bring their guns or their firearms to Starbucks stores. And it worked.

By politely requesting that our customers respect our request, not to bring their firearms to our stores, they were inclined to actually respect our request versus challenge a ban. If you draw a double yellow line, a lot of Second Amendment folks might try to challenge that ban. But by respectfully requesting that folks, when they came into our home or into our stores, respect our requests, that created a whole different atmosphere and tonality to a situation.

So, months, and even years after that decision, guns essentially vanished from Starbucks stores. Other major brands, like Target, called us wanting to understand how we addressed this issue. We joked on the corporate communications team, we could have started a consultancy around how to effectively do this. Many of them actually followed our lead.

In the beginning, it was essentially like most issues that companies face in that they view it through the lens of a binary issue. It's a black and white decision, or it's Option A versus Option B. We got stuck in this treadmill of debate. Then we challenged ourselves to think, is there a third way?

That's the big lesson from this—when you think an issue is only a binary issue, and there's only two choices or two ways out, there are more. I always now challenge myself and my teams going forward every time at any organization. When what appears to be a binary issue appears, I challenge the group to think, okay guys, we're looking at this through these two lenses, but is there a third way? Are we thinking imaginatively enough about how we can work through this issue?

One thing we might have done differently is we should have actually started that debate and made that decision much sooner. We waited for that catalyzing event, Lauren Rousseau's death. In hindsight, there's no reason why we couldn't have, as an organization, started the review of this issue sooner and made that decision sooner.

Fairness Ethics Advice

Fairness and ethics apply to society as a whole. **Marcy Massura,** CEO of MM & Company, believes that our private communication infrastructure may be creating an inherently unethical playing field.

I am concerned about how the private sector is acting as public infrastructure and that's a bit of the nightmare. We have social platforms, cloud providers, and Google. They all can manipulate results to drive knowledge paths, and they can drive actions through preference.

If we can't fix for those things, then it becomes a battle of money, and that's the big concern here. If the bad guys have more money than you, they can win public opinion, and it's scary. I must tell you, it's not something that I feel is compatible without, God forbid, I can't believe these words are coming out of my mouth, some sort of regulation. Some sort of approval on private sector infrastructures.

I am not sure what type, but I just get more uneasy with the unchecked-ness of it all. We're relying on these little soundbites and press releases from Facebook or Google to say, "No, we're doing it good now." It just feels very odd. It's a bit like going to a teacher when you're a kid and saying, "Trust me. I did my homework. It was awesome." But that concerns me more because that's the source of the river of horribleness downstream. We need to start to look at the source in some way that is not handicapping the private sector, but at the same time, assuring some sort of ethical compliance or fairness.

One of the larger fairness ethical issues of our time is cancel culture. **Paul Omodt**, APR, Fellow PRSA, Principal of Omodt and Associates, shares his thoughts:

> The piling on onto social issues ethically is something that we have to look at. There is a growing "cancel culture." It's very easy to go to social media and say, this person did something wrong, and therefore, they should never work ever again.
>
> There's an ethical component to that as a communicator. We are not allowing other people to recover or to do the things they need to do to make amends because the cancelation is so fast. I believe in the idea of people seeking forgiveness and asking for forgiveness and getting redemption when they prove that they deserve it.
>
> But some people think that person should be canceled forever. Human beings are capable of change and capable of doing good things in their lives after they've done something wrong. We've been too fast to cancel people forever.
>
> I may be an outlier in that, but I do see instances where good people have gone down for things, and I don't know that it's fair to them with a personal, not a professional transgression. I sometimes think the bullying goes a little too far. There is not an open checkbook for you to cancel a person out.
>
> Do we allow people the chance to admit that they made a mistake, and it's a new world out there? Maybe what we did 20 years ago or even two years ago was not the right approach, and we need a new one. But do they get canceled forever?

Silicon Valley presents some unique fairness challenges according to **Bryan Scanlon,** Principal of Look Left Marketing:

> There's a lot of money right now for companies, and any time that there's money involved, ethics gets involved. You found a dollar on the street. Pick it up. What do you do with it? That basic ethical debate that is exacerbated when we are dealing with hundreds of millions of dollars.

The second macro thing is there is this incredible and very dangerous work culture that has emerged in Silicon Valley, where if you're not always working, and always connected, and always at the next party to network, and always available 24×7, you're somehow acting irresponsibly in the gold rush. Let's be clear. There's clearly a technology gold rush happening right now. And if you're not mining every day, then you're somehow missing out. There are people I know who basically don't sleep, or they're always on their phones.

I think, as a business owner—Are people getting enough time off? Are they getting enough connections? Can't one person be in on call the old-fashioned way? There is a doctor on call, and that's the doctor who's just going to handle this thing if something comes up. This worries me, because people burn out quickly, and then they start making mistakes. Some of those mistakes are going to be ethical.

The third macro issue is privacy. There are enormous companies in the world who control and have an enormous amount of personal information. We are at this watershed moment of, what do you do with that information? How do you collect it? Who do you share it with? And how do you use it?

If you think about us as marketers, we've always thought about, what's our traffic like? How do we get the numbers up? How do we get more leads in? We need to collect more e-mails so that I can go to sales and show them all these leads that we've had. It creates this arms race where the chart always has to go up to the right. That that's a bit broken. We need to think about, well, why are we collecting this data? And what am I going to give somebody in return?

If we're going to use that data to market, how are we giving something of value to people? There has been this great movement to inbound marketing, but it has also created this very dangerous thing where you're just gathering e-mails, pulling in these nets of giant e-mail addresses. Quite frankly, we've reached the point where the oceans have gotten over fished. We've gathered too much of that data, and now we're responsible for it.

I've seen companies do wonderful things where every three or four months, they have the guts to send a note out to say, "How are we doing? Do you want to stay on our list? Is any of this content useful to you?" And if somebody says no, they let them go. Two years ago, that was unheard of.

To fix this you have to set expectations pretty early on clients, pick good clients, and not be afraid to say, "Listen, this is just not for us. The chemistry's not right."

I find myself, sometimes, telling clients, "We're just closed tomorrow. It's a holiday. I am here if something urgent comes up. Just text me." But it's hard, because there's a time element in public relations. There's this notion of seizing the moment.

A very good photographer friend of mine has taught me that there's always another moment. If you miss a picture, there will be another sunrise. There will be another moment where a dad picks up a child and puts him on their shoulders, and there's this intimate moment to take a picture of. There will always be another moment. But in business, we said that that's never the case, but there will be. I want to be clear, though, you still have to jump on those moments when you see them. You still have to be looking for them and do that.

Technology and AI create fairness issues around ethics. **Brandi Boatner**, IBM, shares her advice on avoiding unconscious bias:

Bias impacts pretty much everything that we do because everyone has beliefs about various things. But we can see unconscious bias in recent campaigns and ads.

A lot of companies have unconscious bias training. There has been a rash of CDOs popping up because of ethical dilemmas from unconscious bias created by a group of people who are sitting in a room coming up with a campaign and there's nobody there to say, "I don't know if this is the right thing that we should be doing."

We need to have an infusion of inclusion. Say that three times real fast.

An inclusion infusion. You have to create a culture of inclusion to help with conscious awareness. Every week we are reading about a chief diversity officer being hired because this happened, there was backlash from this or from that. This continues to happen. Having an infusion of inclusion is one way to fight this. Rome wasn't built in a day so I'm not saying it will stop overnight, but one way to change this behavior if we truly promote more inclusivity.

Five Key Takeaways

How do we maintain the highest standards of fairness?

1. The *New York Times* test is a great guide to making fair, ethical decisions.
2. You won't make everyone happy. That is okay, as long as the decisions were reached fairly.
3. DEI goes beyond fairness, but it sure is a good start.
4. Actively seek out other opinions.
5. You never go wrong following the no A-hole rule.

CHAPTER 8

Free Flow of Information

The free flow of information is essential to ethical public relations. Yet, PR professionals regularly struggle with this. What do they have to share and how much?

The PRSA Code of Ethics gives great guidance:

> ***Free Flow of Information***: "Protecting and advancing the free flow of accurate and truthful information is essential to serving the public interest and contributing to informed decision-making in a democratic society."
>
> The intent is to maintain the integrity of relationships with the media, government officials, and the public and to aid informed decision-making.
>
> A member shall:
>
> Preserve the integrity of the process of communication.
>
> Be honest and accurate in all communications.
>
> Act promptly to correct erroneous communications for which the practitioner is responsible.
>
> Preserve the free flow of unprejudiced information when giving or receiving gifts by ensuring that gifts are nominal, legal, and infrequent.

This chapter takes a deeper look at that issue. But we start off with a larger theme—the importance of civility and civil discourse within the free flow of information. **Emmanuel Tchividjian,** former Chief Ethics Officer for Ruder Finn, explains:

If you don't have civility, you'll have unrest, you'll have violence. It's a deterioration of our core values. In the PR profession, lack of civility is a barrier to communication. We have to relearn it. We have lost the level of civility we had in America in the 1950s and even the 1960s. We have to get back there. We have to rebuild that notion that we're all human beings, we all have blood in our veins. We may disagree, we may have different points of view, but before all, we're human beings on this planet.

To rebuild these bridges, we should go beyond our immediate circles because we're building silos. We read what people we like say, and we ignore what others say or, when we do address them, we confront. We should be open-minded, even if we disagree. We should learn to listen again.

Free Flow of Information in Action

Gary McCormick, APR, Fellow PRSA, discusses how to use the free flow of information to build bridges:

My biggest ethical challenge has been facing the extreme controversy and poignant criticism from activists that questioned my own character and truthfulness in working with communities. It came with the turf, and even though they didn't know me or my work, they attacked my client with an intended outcome that they wanted to achieve. I'm not saying that their outcome was not a good outcome or wasn't an achievable outcome, but the manner in which they did it sometimes questioned my ethics and performance.

I had to maintain my professionalism, not take those attacks personally, and continue to reaffirm and commit that we were doing the right thing, communicating with the citizens, representing their interests with my client, and not reacting personally in the attacks. It was a very challenging time almost any time we got into the communities, one on one or in a public meeting.

For people dealing with this, regardless of what you think of their opinion or their outcome, you must sit down and have a discussion with them. There has to be a two-way dialogue. That's the only way that you can bring some information to the conversation that may help them to understand either the time or science constraints and what has been done and the data that you already have. Many times, there's a reaction before there's a review of the data, because people don't understand the scientific data, and they're defensive because they don't. They don't want to feel as though they're not intelligent or not capable. This is human nature. Anything that we don't understand, we tend to react negatively to. We reflexively think you're not better than I am, or you don't know more than me, or you don't live here, you're not responsible.

You have to get past a lot of the emotional barriers to communication. If you're willing to just sit and listen and continue to provide support and justify that they have every right to get the information because this can impact their lives. You need to affirm that you will help their information get to the right people and get the answers. You have to become a liaison, not a representative for the client.

That's one of the things in environmental work that we make very clear when we start with a client. While you're paying me, you need to understand that I'm a liaison to the community. I am the way in which they get a seat at the table with you to talk about their concerns and for us to address them and to move forward to the outcome that protects everyone.

At first, it's difficult because it's not the way they are used to doing business. One of the things I tell a lot of the communities is that I've worked with a lot of these people in a lot of environmental organizations. All of these people come to work every day to do a good job. They are passionate about what they do, or they wouldn't have gone into this type of work. They're not trying to do wrong things or bad things. They are trying to do the best job they can.

What we need to understand is what are the outcomes that are the most favorable to this community and the client can deliver? Because sometimes, the science is not there, yet for what they would like. The other thing is it takes a long time to do most environmental cleanup, just like it's been a legacy to get to that point. Most of these environmental issues have built up over decades, and it won't go away overnight, and that's very frustrating for communities. It is important to make the client understand that they are going to have to work through these frustrations, and it's going to take time. I tell them if I look as though I'm just speaking for you, there will be no communication, and we'll be right back where we started before I came to the table.

Paul Omodt, APR, Fellow PRSA, Principal of Omodt and Associates, states that speed is not always your ally in the free flow of information:

It's become so easy to communicate so rapidly. At the same time, the level of our societal discourse has become bifurcated. There are two big tribes of with similar social political views. You can make a mistake and blame someone else because that gives you value within your tribe. It's very easy to fall prey to your own trap.

It's very important that people look at, am I communicating what I want to believe and what I do believe? Am I communicating in a way that makes sense to the broadest number of people? In that case, speed can kill you. In crisis response, speed is your ally. But if there is a chance of you doing something stupid, speed is not your ally because you can go virally stupid so fast.

I had a client, a CEO of a major company, right before the 4th of July holiday, who tweeted something in a social political vein thinking it was kind of funny. Kind of a prelude to the 4th of July. Within 10 minutes, the communications director is calling me saying, "Oh my gosh, look at this. How do we go in and fix this?" I said, "First we're going to take a breath."

We're going to both de-escalate because you're escalated. De-escalation is super important because you'll make better ethical decisions when you are calm. You need the check and balance of another person, ideally a friend, to tell you that. I'm the most honest with my friends. My duty as your friend is to be honest with you. A friend will tell you the things that you probably don't want to hear.

Media Relations and External Communication

Where ethics and the free flow of information often come into conflict is in media relations. What do we need to share? How quickly do we need to respond? **Michael Smart**, a leading media relations trainer and coach, elaborates:

> Before I got into training, when I was working in-house as a media relations director, I was serving as a spokesperson on a controversial issue. The organization I represented had put on an activity and an 18-year-old young man tragically died while participating. This was the subject of intense media scrutiny. It turns out that he had directly disobeyed doctor's orders from only a week before not to participate in this very activity, because it would put him at risk.
>
> The media were just all over us about why didn't we have an EMTs stationed at this activity? Why weren't the referees trained in first aid? We decided right away this family was burying their son. They were not criticizing the organization. They were not speaking to the media. They didn't ask for any of the scrutiny.
>
> We said, "We're not going to drag their son through the mud and say, 'You know, he asked for this,'" so we just sat on the news that he had this condition, and that he'd disobeyed doctor's orders. We answered the questions, but we didn't say, "Hey, this isn't our fault. It's because of him."
>
> It seems obvious now, and it was the right thing then, but at the time, we were getting pilloried in the media. As the guy taking those calls, it was frustrating to not be able to say more. Like all media maelstroms, it blew over in a week or two. We were fine, and I'm so glad that we didn't add to what was already a very difficult time for a grieving family.
>
> There are other media relations practices that I see emerging, that demonstrate a clear lack of integrity. Even if you're somebody who doesn't make decisions based on values, they're

counterproductive in terms of getting the long-term results that you want. Specifically:

- It's hard to get reporters' attention via e-mail. So, some people will actually type *Re:* into the subject line, to trick the reporter into thinking that they've already had a conversation with me, that this is part of a thread they've already engaged in, to get them to open the e-mail. That's disingenuous, and while that may work once, your long-term goal is to establish a relationship of trust with that key influencer so you can go back to her again and again, and you're going to fail if the first point of contact is based on a trick.
- There are some other tricks people use where they'll shop exclusive stories to lots of journalists at the same time and just go with the first one that that says yes, and then later act surprised when somebody else runs it. It's a lie and it's going to hurt you in the long run.

We are not the only ones that do this. I was talking to a producer for NBC Nightly News, and she was talking about how hard it is for her to get her e-mails opened within that news organization. She said that when she has a story she wants her senior producer to open, the subject line she uses is "I'm throwing a party for you." Then when they open it, she says, "Not really, but check out this great story. I didn't want you to miss it."

You just need to accept those ethical constraints to prime your creativity and push yourself to get to the types of solutions you haven't engaged previously. Maybe I'll coin a new credo that I'll live by, and that is that an ethical lapse is a lapse of creativity.

Melody Kimmel is the CEO of MKMedia Training, and she goes into more detail on ethics, information, and media interviews:

There's a big difference between spinning, framing, and positioning. You have rights as well as responsibilities in an interview. For starters, it's good for everyone to remember that the news is a constructed product. It doesn't just happen. It's not just this balanced representation of the events of the day. It's balanced based on the input, the resources, the facts that have been gathered. I advise clients to be humble but confident and to own their place in the tale. They have to understand their point of view is legitimate, and it has been perceived by reporters as integral or they wouldn't be asked to participate. We're entitled to tell the story the way we see it, and we can decide which facts to focus on, but we cannot manufacture information.

I believe to my core that truth exists. But it's also important when framing a story, you have to speak up. You have to have your voice heard. If you refuse the interview, or if you take the interview and keep brandishing a very curt no comment, you're relinquishing your space in the story. And no doubt, other people are going to tell it for you, and undoubtedly, it's not going to be the way you would want to tell it or the way you see events.

You need to frame your story. You need to position it. You're not spinning it. You are telling the story as you see it in your own language.

You don't have to tell every single detail. You can use broader brush strokes. I tell people to find the boundary. It's important for us in our private lives to have boundaries, and it's true in public communications as well. It is not your duty to tell the other side of the story, nor is it your appropriate role. It's not your area of expertise. You can only speak for the part of the story that you control or that you're responsible for. You don't want to speculate. You don't want to guess. And you don't want to speak for another company or another individual.

Most of us in PR are familiar with blocking and bridging. I am a fan of that. It's a deft and legit way to make it clear that what you've just been asked about is not in your area of expertise and to bring the conversation back to what you are expert in talking about. There's nothing wrong with answering a question with something like, "That would be a better question for them. What I can tell you about is blank," or "I'm at the Acme Company and the way we approach blank is as follows." Stick with what you know. Find the line.

Even in a crisis, people and brands need to remain authentic, to stay true to their brand identity. They need to be transparent, and they need to act and communicate quickly.

If nature abhors a vacuum, so does the public and so does all types of media. The public is going to evaluate companies by asking, "What do you know? When did you learn it? What did you do about it?" If you made a mistake, own it. That will support reputation repair nearly as much as not having made the mistake in the first place. When you make a mistake, own it and fix it.

I do my best to follow my own advice. I look to the four Rs as a process to follow—regret, restitution, reform, and responsibility. Express regret that something happened that fell short of what you expect of this brand. Restitution, give back, make whole in any way you possibly can. By the way, not all of this can happen on day one of a crisis.

Reform. What are we going to do differently to keep this from happening again? That wouldn't be credible if it were announced on Day 1. The Day 1 story version of reform might be, "We are doing a root cause analysis." Figure out if there's something we can do better, improve, so this never happens again.

And the fourth R is responsibility. Take it throughout, sound like you are shouldering the blame and the responsibility for getting to the bottom of what happened, making people whole and fixing it.

Starbucks is a great example. It was almost exactly two years ago; they had a bad misfire, and we can barely remember it now. The manager in a Philadelphia store called the police on two African American men who were sitting in the store without having ordered anything. They said they were waiting for friends to show up, who indeed did show up a little while later. That was two years, and 11 million views of the Twitter video ago.

Well, what did Starbucks do after this dreadful episode? Quickly Starbucks parted ways with the store manager. Soon after the CEO came to Philadelphia, apologized to the gentlemen, and a month after the incident, Starbucks did something that was unprecedented at that time. They closed their 8,000 U.S. stores for one day to conduct racial bias education for 175,000 employees.

Now let's fast-forward two years when the police murders of George Floyd and other innocent black people have assaulted a community already staggering from the quarantine's disproportionate health and economic blows. Starbucks is one of the companies that issued a public letter. It supported Black Lives Matter, and it encouraged what they called courageous conversations. Nobody has responded by invoking a snarky mention of the earlier crisis, because as I see it, their actions had allowed them to get past that.

Scott Monty, a neoclassical digital executive who led Ford's digital and social media, takes this a step further and discusses the perils of obfuscation:

A lot of business schools teach ethics, but it tends to be fairly theoretical. It isn't until you sit down, and you're faced with something, and it smacks you … it's not as black and white as you might see in a case study. It just kind of creeps up on you.

There was an occasion where our communications team was addressing a safety issue and used a term that very clearly would not be a term that normal people would throw around in conversation and euphemistically referenced what would commonly be called a fire.

It was referred to in the communications team as a *thermal incident*, and we were expected to go out and talk with people about this and to use that as our official message. I basically said, "Are you kidding me with this? I can't with a straight face use the term 'thermal incident' when everybody is already talking about fire." There are certainly legal implications there, and it had to be handled with a wink and a nudge, but also with an acknowledgment that I knew where the concern was coming from.

Quentin Langley, author of Brandjack, wonders if ethical PR pros can follow the "do not lie" maxim in media relations.

We just had a debate in my class at FIT about if a PR professional should never lie for a client.

Most students chose to speak in favor of never lying. Many of them cite PRSA's Code of Ethics and focused on the meaning of the word professional. The students that spoke against picked up on the word, never. Which is of course a very tough word, and they cited examples of protecting a client's privacy.

For example, if your client was a gay NBA player who didn't want to come out in the locker room to his colleagues, then you have a very, very strict obligation of confidentiality and privacy there, which would be intentioned with your obligation of transparency. As a professional, you have to wrestle with that.

The closest I've ever come to lying for a client would be a secretarial lie, "No, I'm afraid she's not available at the moment." When what I mean is I told her not to be available, this would be a stupid interview to do.

There was a case years ago. A cabinet member was being quizzed by a select committee of the British Parliament that asked, "Are there ever any circumstances in which a Minister could lie to the House of Commons?" He said, "Yes," and he got in trouble for that. Ironically, of course, he was getting into trouble for telling the truth. Sometimes you do have to lie. He gave the example of a Foreign Secretary, years earlier, who had made a clear statement in the House of Commons and publicly, about a couple, who had been arrested traveling in Eastern Europe in the Warsaw Pact and accused of spying. The Foreign Secretary made a statement, that "These people are not spies, they're just innocent businesspeople." In fact, they were spies, as it turned out years later.

But of course, they would be exposed to execution and torture if the government confirmed that they were spies. So of course, he said that they weren't. So, you can always raise the stakes and say, "Well, what happens if you tell the truth here, and sometimes what happens can be disastrous."

Kelly Davis, APR, Fellow PRSA, Public Relations Sequence Head at the University of South Carolina, highlights how to avoid landmines and understand the fine lines of free flow of information in public affairs and lobbying:

I spent five years working as a consultant to a national non-profit advocacy organization to pass tobacco control policy in

South Carolina. As you can imagine, in a southern, traditional tobacco-producing state, it is definitely a controversial and touchy subject. We have not only that history of tobacco production as a major crop in South Carolina, but also the legacy of the tobacco brands' sponsorships in local communities. We have conservative philosophies about taxes, and our organization's main focus was cigarette taxes.

Public policy and legislative work involves a lot of landmines and fine lines around ethics, to be sure that you're following the state ethics laws and guidelines as well as your personal codes of ethics and consideration. I was managing a very broad coalition with a lot of partners and was trying to keep everybody on the same page about what were the right decisions to make, what was going to be appropriate, and where are the things that we needed to avoid.

You always have to be very clear about the line between lobbying and advocacy. It's a line in the sand, and you've got to stay on the advocacy side. We worked with contract lobbyists as well as the staff lobbyists for the organizations who were part of our coalition. They handled the lobbying activities, while most of our coalition members were engaged in the advocacy and education side. You need to constantly consider which side of that line you're on, being very mindful of the information that you can and can't share, who you can talk to and who you can't, what you can say and what you can't.

We worked with grassroots advocates all over the state, gathering their stories, their experiences, why these issues were so important to them, and had to maintain confidentiality where it was needed versus just saying, "Hey, would you like to come and be the spokesperson, or testify in front of a committee?" We had to continually balance what was appropriate and what was disrespectful, based on that person's experience and their story.

One of the biggest ethical challenges when you're working at tobacco control is you're up against a very well-funded, and not always honest, opponent. The tobacco companies and the many, many, many lobbyists that they employed in our state.... It's kind of like David and Goliath, trying to get our message out there and knowing that we had such a well-funded opponent with very deep and very strong relationships, both with legislators and grassroots civil advocates around the state.

You have to do what's best for your client as well as what's best for the community. It is the proudest work of my career. I was very gratifying that we were able to pass the legislation in 2010, and now 10 years later, we can look at data that shows that we saw significant declines in smoking rates among youth, our primary focus, as well as a decline in adult smoking rates as well.

Free Flow of Information Ethics Advice

John Walker, Founder and Managing Partner of Chirp PR, shares how the free flow of information can build trust in a time of uncertainty.

The future is quite uncertain right now, because so many companies shut down their marketing communications over the pandemic. Those companies that did not lead will find a slower return to market normalcy. Their long-term reputation will be impacted because they did not communicate with compassion and empathy. They went quiet without letting their customers, their employees, their stakeholders know that we're here, and we are going to navigate this together.

I highlighted the challenges of cancel culture in other chapters, and **Tim O'Brien**, APR, Founder of O'Brien Communications and host of the Shaping Opinion podcast, highlights how deplatforming impacts the free flow of information:

The First Amendment is in play and deplatforming concerns me.

When you're doing issues work, oftentimes you have two sides on an issue, and there's a strategy of deplatforming, a calculated effort by some, to frame their opponents as fringe. To marginalize them, to silence them by getting them removed from digital platforms like Facebook.

The difference between real hate speech and real lying is something we know. But in this case, when people use it as a strategy, they are positioning themselves as self-appointed speech enforcers. They broaden the definition of what should be prohibited speech to suit their own strategies. For example, recently, the Harvard Crimson ran a story about protests over the federal ICE department. The student newspaper, the Harvard Crimson, covered the protests against ICE. They tried to interview ICE. They didn't get a response, so they said, "ICE could not be reached for comment."

The students protesting ICE, turned on the newspaper and went after the newspaper through a petition. They said that the newspaper should never have even approached ICE for comment. That became an issue. It escalated, and some of the larger news media picked up on it.

That's an extreme example, but there are people who want to deny those who oppose them the chance to speak. And they do it by attacking them in ways that may not always be accurate.

The key to dealing with speech you don't like is more speech. And unless it's truly defamatory, unless it's truly slanderous, we have to respect the First Amendment.

There is speech out there that's ugly. It's not speech that we would respect in any way, but that doesn't mean it's our job to seek to silence them. Once you do that, then where do you draw the line?

Maybe more importantly, who should be given the power to deny speech? Do we want that to be in the hands of the government, another special interest, somebody that opposes us, a politician, or a company? Do we want the digital platforms deciding what speech is okay or not? And how do they do that? What criteria do they use?

It's a slippery slope. I started in journalism, and I feel that the First Amendment is sacred. As ugly as it is when people sometimes exercise their free speech, I still think having the freedom of speech is something we need to protect.

To stop this takes a little bit of courage. It's the old see something, say something adage. If you see someone's trying to deny someone else their right to free speech, it's almost incumbent on us as communicators to speak up. We have a lot of say in what goes on our social channels and our websites. There may be times when people say things, or want to say things through our platforms, that others want to silence. We have to allow that, as much is reasonable.

If it's on our own channels, like a Facebook group that we control, and someone's being truly disrespectful, yes that might need to be moderated. But in other cases, we have to respect freedom of speech, because we don't want anyone to do the same to us.

There's a code of ethics for people that run social media sites. If you delete that comment, that's breaking a major rule. And in a lot of cases, under normal circumstances, that is.

But when you're dealing with an extraordinary circumstance, there may be times to be more active in moderating your own channels, because you have to think of that greater good we talked about. Is this going to hurt the organization? Is this going to hurt somebody else?

The criteria are, is the speech slanderous or libelous? Does it break any kind of compliance rule? Is there a material disclosure? Is there something that might fly against the regulations of the FTC or some other group? Does it include information that is proprietary or protected or confidential?

Most forums have rules. You must respect others, and there mustn't be any profanity or name-calling. Enforce those to allow for a more constructive dialogue. But if someone simply disagrees with you, and if they're able to do it respectfully and ethically and honestly, we need to try to safeguard that to the extent that we can.

Our natural inclination is to not want to address mistakes or bury them under the rug. **Krista Terrell**, APR, Acting President of the Arts and Science Council for Charlotte Mecklenburg County, discusses why the free flow of information is the best approach to convince executives to report historic inequities:

To address equity moving forward, to nourish an equitable creative ecosystem requires us to be transparent.

It all goes back to being honest and showing the data and the facts.

There's a John Meacham quote I love, and it says, "History is not a GPS. It is a diagnostic guide." Everyone loves to talk about the shiny new things. But you have to start at the beginning. You have to start with history and be honest about that and see what you have done to know how to move forward. Everything starts with history.

Michelle Egan, APR, Fellow PRSA, Chief Communications Officer of the Alyeska Pipeline Service Company, also discusses how we need to fight the attack on the free flow of information:

We must protect the free flow of information.

As we start to see confirmation bias takeover and people have so many choices in the media and information they consume, we are getting in a position as citizens that we're seeing only one side of an issue.

As public relations practitioners, the challenge is to try to present both sides, even though your organization does have a perspective. It's harder in a private organization like the one I'm in now to see that than it is where I was before in a school district where you don't have a choice. It is your obligation.

We must guard against people receiving only one side of a story. How can we expect people in our society to make good choices when they don't know all sides of an issue? As this advances and accelerates, it feels like we often don't know where the truth lies. Then add disinformation and you've got a much more complicated situation.

We must continue to seek out different perspectives. We have to work extra hard to get out and listen to the other side. If your company is trying to advance a particular idea or product, it's easy to stay in your echo chamber and hear from all the people who support it and think it's a great idea, and then try to influence people who are on the periphery of that. But we have to spend time with people who are critics. People who disagree with us.

We have to listen and build relationships there. If we can't do that, if we can't be inclusive and transparent, we're unable to do our job. Not only is it an ethics issue, it's harmful to our companies.

Five Key Takeaways

How do we maintain the free flow of information?

1. Bad news does not get better with time.
2. Admitting mistakes goes a long way to building trusted relationships.
3. The best response to attacks and disinformation is correct information.
4. Would you want to know more? If so, the odds are key stakeholders would as well.
5. Speed is a double-edged sword. Ready, fire, aim is not the correct approach.

CHAPTER 9

Competition

Competition is the lifeblood of business. We compete with other companies, agencies, and employees. The desire to get ahead can lead many to skirt the ethical line.

PRSA's Code of Ethics states:

> Promoting healthy and fair competition among professionals preserves an ethical climate while fostering a robust business environment.
>
> The intent is to promote respect and fair competition among public relations professionals and to serve the public interest by providing the widest choice of practitioner options.
>
> Some guidelines include following ethical hiring practices designed to respect free and open competition without deliberately undermining a competitor and preserving intellectual property rights in the marketplace.

Ethics and Competition in Action

This chapter takes a deeper look at ethical issues that come up in competition.

New Business

For agency executives, nowhere does this come to light more than in the pursuit of new business.

Dave Close, the retired Managing Director of MSL Boston, elaborates:

> A tremendous amount of energy is spent feeding the machine and acquiring new clients. There are ethical challenges in the endless pitching process. I can recall several instances where we probably

could have won a big client assignment if we had been willing to make promises that we probably ultimately couldn't fill. Or agree to client requests or requirements in their RFP that we knew we couldn't fulfill, and probably couldn't be done. There were cases where we didn't win a new client because one of our competitors had promised them things that we knew they couldn't deliver.

One was a relatively low fee assignment that we didn't win. I asked why and they said, "this other agency promised us four vice presidents on our team." That is not going to happen.

Most agencies keep things very ethical and honest in the pitch process because that's going to set the tone for the entire relationship. If you start the relationship on a set of false or unreasonable promises or impossible expectations, it's not going to go well.

There's a famous saying in the open-source software world, "Information wants to be free." Not as in free beer, but it wants to be set free, information will have freedom. That applies to the truth as well in any kind of communications or messaging effort. The truth will set itself free. There's never anything to be gained in the long run by trying to trim or alter the facts.

Ken Hunter, President and Chief Strategist at The PowerStation, discusses what to do when your boss makes unethical promises during a new business pitch:

I didn't say anything the first time I heard an unethical promise in a pitch, but in the car drive back to the office, I mentioned to that boss that there's no way that the story ideas they talked about in this meeting are going to be appropriate for *The Wall Street Journal.* He was like, it doesn't matter, we're just trying to sell them on hiring us and whatever it takes to close the deal. I said, I understand with new business that there is a degree of salesmanship. However, as a public relations person, even if my roommates from college were all the top editors at *The Wall Street Journal,* there's no way I could ever guarantee the story being covered.

There are way too many factors that will impact it. Some prospects that will say, "We want to be in a lot of top media." It's very important to honestly tell them, here's why you're not there yet. If that's where you aspire to be, we're going to have to take steps to get you there. It's not just me with a connection. Let me call my old college roommate and he'll be happy to run this story. That's not how it works. Plus, it's unethical if I put my friend in that place if I say, look, I have a client that's breathing down my back.

It goes beyond your connections. Many times, I'll hear, "We want to be on the Today Show." But probably one half of 1 percent of *Today Show* viewers are the target audience. I ask if this is a potential piece that's more for your ego or is it going to be better for your stockholders, your investors, your employees to be able to look at a much less glamorous trade publication. Usually, you can win that argument for short time, but then eventually, they'll get the stars in their eyes and say, are we ready yet for our big, big close up, Mr. Demille…

Angela Sinickas, CEO of Sinickas Communications, highlights three ethical missteps with the proposal process.

Some of them are kind of clichés, but they're still a wrong.

- One of the clichés is that when you're hiring a PR firm or an agency, you meet different people. They typically send you the senior people, and then if you hire them, you might never see that senior person again. You're going to be working with a junior person you may never have met.
  The cliché is that people sort of say, "Well that's what you should expect." But that's wrong. Yes, you should still have the senior people going to those proposal meetings, but you should bring in the junior people who will be the actual project managers so that the client gets a chance to see, do we have a good personality connection here? Is this someone I can work with? Because that's who they're going to be having to work with.
- Another thing is I see people bidding on projects they're in no way competent to do. I do research and measurement full time. At first, I noticed that PR firms would start doing

employee communication consulting, not using specialists and employee communication, just saying, "Hey look, we can do this too. It's just communication. What's the big difference?" Or they would start doing research even though they had no research background. How hard can it be to just put together a survey on SurveyMonkey? They'd bid on things they had no capability to do.

It's an easy fix too, if you want to expand into that direction, you hire someone with that skill, or you get a subcontractor to work with you in doing that kind of project. It's so easy to avoid this type of bait and switch.

- The big elephant in the room is cost estimates for proposals. When I create proposal estimates, I provide very clear assumptions. If these are the number of questions we have on the survey, the number of languages, online only or online and print…. Given these assumptions, this is what the range will be, and it will not be exceeded.

  A lot of times, to win people will come in with a low-ball bid and not put all those assumptions in there. Then they go into the project planning meeting…. Oh, you wanted more than 10 questions on your survey? Well then, the budget has to be much higher.

  That's slimy. But they do it to get the foot in the door. And at that point, the client is probably going to keep working with them because they've made a commitment and people don't like to admit that they've made a mistake.

  If you happen to be a vendor whose budgets maybe are a little bit higher … explain why. Say, "This is what you would typically get from another vendor. But the way I do this work, you get not only this report, but you get this report, this report, and you get recommendations." Explain what they get for that additional value, and if they don't want all that additional value, then you can reduce your own costs.

Marisa Vallbona, Founder and President of CIM, Inc. PR, discusses what to do when people steal your ideas:

I was ethics officer for the San Diego chapter of PRSA and I was called frequently to police ethical challenges. There were four that were quite frankly pretty shocking.

1. I was called about an individual who started spreading rumors about the owner of a PR firm so that the employees would leave that firm. Then he would recruit those employees. They were malicious lies. The owner of the PR firm contacted me when he found out that this was happening, and he reported it to me as ethics officer. I contacted the person who was spreading these lies. The person, of course, denied it, but we had proof. I contacted the employees who had been the recipient of these malicious rumors, and we got to the bottom of it.

2. An agency submitted work and passed it off as their own when clearly it belonged to someone else. Clearly, it was copyright infringement, and that just blew me away.

3. There was an employee who silently collected data while employed by her agency. And then, she did everything she could to sabotage that agency. She was discovered and fired.

4. An agency was just getting started, and they contacted me, and said, "We would like to hire you as a consultant because we're fascinated by what you did, founding PR Consultants Group. We want to hire you as a consultant to learn what you did because we want to understand that model." I told them, "Okay, this is proprietary information. I'm not going to give you the exact model, but I'll explain to you what we did." I didn't share with them exactly what we did. I gave them the bare skeleton of it.

Two months later, this PR firm launched using our exact model. They used our map of the United States. They used the exact tagline that we had. We had to file a lawsuit against them for trademark infringement. What just blows me away is how, I don't want to say how stupid people are, but how they just don't think.

You know what? I do want to say that. They just don't think things through. They're not inventive enough or confident enough in their own capabilities to do their own work. They have to steal other people's work. It's crazy.

When I uncover IP theft, in the past, I've been kind enough to contact the individual and say, "This is my work." Unfortunately, I have found that it doesn't always work. So, I also have a good corporate attorney who writes, as we say in Texas, "Bless your heart" letters, and that seems to work.

I had a situation once that blew me away. An individual tapped a few members of the PR Consultants Group when she was starting her agency. There were a few of us who collectively had won a few PRSA Silver Anvil awards. She thought, okay, this is going to be a great way for me to get in and get some new business. She was good at getting new business.

But what was interesting is, she put on her website that she had these clients, that she had won these Silver Anvil awards. When we discovered that, we asked her, please take this down. You did not have these clients. These were not your clients. These are not your Silver Anvils. You can say that some of the members of your team have worked with these clients. Some of the members of your team have won these Silver Anvils, but you can't say that you did. She didn't see the distinction.

Steve Cody, Founder and CEO of Peppercomm, also highlights ethical failures with IP theft and RFPs.

I hate to say it, but it's an easy way to get new ideas. If the pressure is on, and you don't have the budget, and you don't necessarily have a moral compass, it's pretty tempting to do an agency search, have them come in, give you some great ideas, and then come back and say, "Geez, you know what? The budget that we thought had been approved in November, it's still being debated, so we'll get back to you," and you never hear from them again. There's still a tremendous amount of that going on. It's not being policed, and it should be.

Ad Age did a big expose on it, but it's happening all the time in PR. It's as if it doesn't even exist. You will not find articles in *PR Week* or *Holmes* about it. It's like it's not happening, but yet it's happening to every single agency, and we're losing time, money, and intellectual property, the whole nine yards. Somebody's got to step up at some point. If one big agency draws the line in the sand and says, "No more. You're going to pay us for our ideas. We're going to come in and present them. If you don't like them, that's fine, but we're getting paid."

"Well, four other agencies said they didn't need to be paid, so if you're insisting on being paid, we're not going to let you pitch the business."

"Okay, fine." At least you've put the line in the sand. We're going to start doing that as much as possible. I mean, if we do get a Google or a Facebook asking us to pitch, maybe we'll waive that proviso, but if it's Joe and Bob's Tree Nursery asking us to go up to Nashua, New Hampshire, to pitch against three other firms, I am not going to do it, unless they pay our way and pay for our ideas.

We've instituted that, over the last couple of years as much as we can. Companies respect it. They're not happy, but they respect it. Some of them are very taken aback and will say, "No other agency has asked that."

My typical response is, "Well, not every agency is Pepper-comm." They'll come back, and typically they'll say, "We'll meet you halfway."

If it's a good. If it plays to our sweet spot, and they're willing to meet us halfway, in terms of the out-of-pocket cost, we'll go. If they say, "No, you've got to pay," we just won't do it.

Another failure ethically is who is in the room for a new business pitch. We end all of our new business pitches by saying, "I hate to break it to you, but what you see is what you'll get." I don't bring in people from central casting, who were press secretaries and former governors. We don't play that game. We don't bring in the A-team and dazzle the prospect, and then if we are fortunate enough to win, all of a sudden, they've got a 24-year-old, a 26-year-old, and a 22-year-old.

We win quite a bit of business by picking up the pieces after an organization has been burned by a bait and switch. It catches up to you big time, and you get a reputation within the corporate world when the CEOs gather together.

Competition and Personal Values

Another issue with competition is balancing the desire to bring in revenue with the desire to only work with clients you believe in. **Erin Callanan**, APR, Director of Media Relations for GBH, explains:

> You have to trust your gut. If it doesn't feel good, don't go there. You have a responsibility to your employees to bring the business in and to ensure that they're getting paid every month. To do that, you have to have clients. But there are clients out there where their story isn't quite as solid as it should be. You know instinctively, if it doesn't feel right, it's going to be a hard client to support. You have to trust your instincts on that.
>
> I don't think that a lot of clients are intentionally trying to lead people wrong. They look at PR and don't understand how important it is to be truthful, accurate, and honest, and how that will help them grow.
>
> If it doesn't feel right, your client goes away unhappy, you feel unhappy. Nobody wins in that process. I learned the hard way a couple of times, but you must trust your instincts.

David Calusdian, President of Sharon Merrill Associates, elaborates further:

> When I look back at the most difficult ethical challenge I ever confronted, I go back to before I got into IR. I was in grad school as a political communication major, and I was trying to get candidate clients for a nascent political consulting business that my friend and I wanted to start. We were introduced to a great candidate who was running in a primary to capture a seat from an opponent who we really wanted to unseat. This guy was smart, well spoken, had a stellar record in the community, and really cared about doing a good job for the people. He wasn't on an ego trip. He wanted to make a difference, and he was some-body that we liked. We thought we could make a difference in this campaign.

Then we found out he was on the wrong side of one particular issue that we both really cared about, and we faced a tough choice. Do we not take this business that would be great for us professionally and work with this guy who, other than this one issue, was a great candidate who lined up with us politically? We spoke with friends and family, and in the end, didn't take him on. That one issue was just too important to us.

I always come back to that story because it shows how it wasn't a black or white issue. This guy was a quality guy. He just was not lined up with us completely. Thinking about politics, it's not like you're getting married to the candidate. It's more like getting on a bus and going in the right direction with someone. When you're working with a client, you need to think about does the company overall reflect your values. Can you do a good job for the client and know that at the end of the day you've contributed to the greater good?

Ironically, we ended up working with a candidate who was totally in line with us, hook, line, and sinker on everything, but was just a terrible candidate. We took the loss on that one, but we're glad we took the route we did. I always think back on that and know that you need to always live your values, and that goes for any client that you're taking on as well.

Cheryl Procter-Rogers, APR, Fellow PRSA, a PR and business strategist, shares an example when she was asked to spread bad information about a competitor:

Often, we don't even realize that we have faced an ethical dilemma until the stuff hits the fan. Then you realize you've stepped in something, and you've got the mud all over your shoes. For me, the most challenging issue was when an executive of an organization I was working for asked me if I would make a call to a reporter at a major publication to spread some bad things about one of the leaders of a competing organization.

At first, I thought it was a joke. When I realized the person was very serious, I didn't know how to position my answer in such a way that I wouldn't get fired immediately, or that worse yet, I would lose credibility. I felt up until that point that I was becoming the go-to person. I was very young in my career, and I just didn't know what to do.

So, I didn't answer right away, which I now realize was a mistake, and I called my mentor, Chester Berger, and told him I felt very uncomfortable, this was not something that I wanted to do. Even though the information may have been true, I had no evidence that that information was true.

I got great advice from Chet, and that is, "Always align with your values, never your bank account."

So, I went back into the office, and I said, "You know, I'm not comfortable doing this. This goes against who I am as a professional, and if that's going to be an issue for you, let me know now." I was not fired, but it was a valuable lesson for me in how I felt that I didn't have the power to say no when in fact I actually did.

If other people find themselves in similar situations, they should they take a deep breath, and if they feel it's important, talk it out with someone.

For the young professional, it's a very scary moment, but do not to feel that you have to respond right away. Much like we say in media interviews, don't be afraid of silence, and take a moment and think it through. If you're having some feeling in your gut, or in your heart, that this is not right, ask for a little time to step away, and consult with a trusted advisor who can give you some guidance, not just on what you should or should not do, but how you should communicate your response to the ask.

Looking back, I realized I didn't have a framework for decision-making then. Without it, I was being very indecisive, and my communication was poor. There are so many different frameworks for decision-making. Google the topic and find a framework that you can use that will help you. For instance, the first thing you're supposed to do is make sure you have sufficient information, and then the knowledge and the skill to make sure that's all aligned.

So, if someone is asking you to do something that is not in line with your background, knowledge, or experience, and it can have a significant impact on your organization, you must speak up and state it. Sometimes, we have this hesitation, especially when we're young, we don't want to seem dumb. We don't want to say we don't know. You should always be transparent and honest and let your manager know that this is not your area of expertise or knowledge.

Next, always think about all the possible outcomes and not just the outcome that you want. Sometimes, with situational ethics, the situation calls for some action, and you could possibly do something terribly wrong, but for a greater good. You must make sure that you're not in that kind of dilemma where you're so focused so that you don't end up saying "Well, you know, all we want to do is make sure all of these starving individuals are able to eat, and the fact that we're stealing the food, well I can't really matter right now."

Yes, it does.

Finally, after you think of all the possible outcomes, make sure that any decision that you're making aligns with your personal values and the values of that organization with which you're working.

Ethics and Competition Advice

When it comes to competition, **Deirdre Breakenridge**, bestselling author, reminds people that we often fail when we make choices alone.

As public relations professionals, I recommend, no matter how noisy it gets, to check your sources and don't make choices alone.

When you make a choice alone, you're putting yourself and your integrity at a risk. At the end of the day, what do you have left? All you have left is your integrity.

Don't make those choices alone. I had a client a while back who actually went to prison and talks about you should never make choices alone. He violated FCPA and anti-bribery laws. When he was in prison, he read my books, and he came out and he needed a new trajectory. He knew he was now making better decisions and he wanted to educate others. Part of his story he shared was he did make choices alone, and that got him into trouble in Third World countries.

You always want to rely on the smartest people around you. So, within your company, bring it out in the open if there are questions. You can question and give people the opportunity to question with you so that you can all make a sound decision. Sometimes, we go to our outside network of confidants who are in our closest circle. There's many a time that I reach out to somebody for a gut check.

That helps. It really does, because sometimes you're in your own bubble and you're moving so quickly. Everybody can say, "Well, maybe I don't have time." But take that two minutes or five minutes, whatever it takes. When reporters are knocking on your door, it's their job to make you answer quickly. They want you to jump on the phone and lose all sight of everything else. Take the 15 minutes, the 20 minutes, the two hours, whatever it is that you need, so you don't make a major mistake.

Tim O'Brien, APR, Founder of O'Brien Associates, believes relative ethics can get business and professionals in trouble when it comes to competition.

There's a mindset in society that ethics are relative.

I was speaking to a group of MBA students recently. It's very realistic for some of the people in this class to envision themselves starting a business and selling it to Google or Uber or Amazon within the next two or three years.

We were having a conversation about crisis communications in the group, and there were students from around the world. One of the students asked me, "Is it okay to lie?"

It was a loaded question on his part, because he had his mind made up. I said, "No, it's never okay to lie." Then he said, "What about other parts of the world, where cultures are different and it's more acceptable to lie?" I said, "What do you mean by that?" And he said, "Well, what you think is lying here, and what someone else might think is lying in another part of the world, may be two different things."

One of the examples he used, because I did probe it, was about how you buy things. In other words, if you go in America to a store, you see a price tag on the item and you buy it. When you go to a market somewhere else, you might bargain or negotiate. So, the vendor might tell you a certain price, but that vendor's always willing to negotiate it.

That was a very simple example. But the student said that way of doing business starts at the local market, but may work its way up into the boardrooms and C-suites too. I didn't agree with him on that, but that was his point of view.

His theory was that if you don't tell people what the pros and cons of a product are, or a piece of software, let's say, then it's up to the buyer to ask the questions and discover what could be wrong with it.

I said to him, "Well, let me ask you this. If your teacher here tells you you're going to get an A, and your teacher gives you a C, is that okay?" That stopped him. He said, "Well, no, that's not okay." There was a little bit of laughter in the class, because all of a sudden, if the lie affected him, it wasn't okay.

That subject has come up in other classes and I've used that example since. It's almost universally a reality check for people who might think that something as fundamental as lying could be okay.

At another school, I saw in a syllabus, "It may be unethical to impose your ethics on others." It was a variation of what this other student said to me, that your ethics are self-determined and are individual to you.

I don't think ethics are relative. Ethics exists to provide a basis or a foundation. These are standards on which we all can agree. They may not be all the standards, but they are at least the baseline standards on which we all agree are right or wrong. They aren't relative, and they're not situational. Because if ethics weren't standard in some way, then there would be chaos.

The biggest challenge in the world of ethics and in communications is to reject the notion that ethical standards are relative. There shouldn't be gray areas. There is a difference between right or wrong. That's one of the things we try to do in PRSA, with the Board of Ethics and Professional Standards. We use our codes of ethics and our codes of conduct as structure to deliver that message.

Scott Monty, a neoclassical digital executive who led Ford's digital and social media, believes many companies are ethically challenged when it comes to competition.

This has been playing out in the news certainly over the last two years or so. We know about the various platforms that we've heard about as far as manipulation of information and even hacking over the course of elections. Facebook looms large in all of this because it is the largest platform out there, but it is also the laxest in its ethical standards. It seems Facebook has, over the course of its short history, been governed by apology. They will put a toe over a certain technical/ethical line, whether it's invasion of privacy or how they deal with your data. Then, there will be a great big blowback, a collective gasp from the online community and Facebook will say, "Our bad, we're sorry." They'll step back, and yet then, they will creep forward eventually back to that step when they think that the storm has blown over.

That's a dangerous way to do business because all they've done is get called on things and then apologize. It's very clear that they're doing quite well as a company and yet they've got people who are in almost sweathouse conditions looking through some of the vilest content online. Casey Newton did big expose on this[1] in *The Verge* about the PTSD that their contractors are going through. The company doesn't seem to have an empathetic bone in its body. It seems very engineering driven and very dispossessed in understanding the human emotional toll that some of these behaviors are taking.

---

[1] C. Newton. February 25, 2019. "The Trauma Floor," *Verge*.

This is where I come back to the classics. Facebook could have done a lot better if it had more liberal arts folks on staff rather than just engineers at its earliest days. There was no one there who understood sociology and psychology at a deeper level, and who understood what the potential implications might be when this rolled out and how humans have acted over time. The stuff that Facebook is exposing now isn't new. This is human behavior that's been embedded in our psyche since time immemorial. It's just amplifying it.

It was Albert Schweitzer who said, "The first step in the evolution of ethics is a sense of solidarity with other human beings." This gets back to customer-centricity. If you're making decisions but you actually aren't going through the purchase process yourself, if you aren't experiencing it through a customer's eyes, if you aren't feeling the same kind of pain that someone feels when something goes wrong, then you truly aren't being empathetic in solidarity with other humans.

Five Key Takeaways

How do we maintain ethical competition?

1. Don't overpromise.
2. What you do today will come back to you tomorrow.
3. Follow Kant's categorical imperative.
4. Don't compromise your standards.
5. Come up with your own ideas

CHAPTER 10

Disclosure of Information

When I have discussions with other professionals, no topic gets more ethical questions than disclosure of information. Transparency is a watchword. But practical transparency can challenge even the most senior pros. We are confidants and counsel, yet we also advocate disclosure. Where do we draw the line?

PRSA states in its Code of Ethics "Disclosure of Information."

The Core Principle is open communication fosters informed decision-making in a democratic society.

The intent is to build trust with the public by revealing all information needed for responsible decision-making.

PRSA offers the following six guidelines

Be honest and accurate in all communications.

Act promptly to correct erroneous communications for which the member is responsible.

Investigate the truthfulness and accuracy of information released on behalf of those represented.

Reveal the sponsors for causes and interests represented.

Disclose financial interest (such as stock ownership) in a client's organization.

Avoid deceptive practices.

Disclosure of Information in Action

Some disclosure issues are straightforward, but some present gray areas. Let's start off with a big one dealing with what you can and cannot disclose. Or as **Robert Johnson**, former Head of TSA Comms asks, when national security is on the line, how do you handle public relations ethically?

My most challenging ethical issue was when I was managing communications after 9/11 for TSA. Americans wanted to know what their government was doing with regard to transportation security, mostly related to aviation. It was my job as the head of that office to explain it to them without giving up secret or top secret information. There was a big worry in the country at that time that there would be another attack, and that it would be just as bad if not worse. How could we keep the economy going without risking some future attack?

My job often was to find a way to inform the media and thus the public about what we were doing without jeopardizing national security. The media never got all that they wanted, but they got a lot more than the TSA people wanted to give them because I was acting on their behalf, trying to balance two very different and competing interests.

Telling the truth and national security. Could it be compromised, should you go too far in telling the truth?

You have to start by convincing them the need to not only communicate something, but that you can do it without giving up too much. I spent a lot of time interfacing with people who had been admirals of the Pacific fleet, commanders of all the tanks in Europe, and all of the B-52 bombers in the Western hemisphere. There were a lot of people leaving very, very high-ranking military jobs to come into aviation to help secure the homeland.

They all had a very strong opinion of what should be done. They all had been in charge. So, here is this kid, compared to them I was 36 or 37 years old, telling them we need to show the media how we're going to train pilots to carry firearms on an airplane because we spent decades trying to get guns out of airplanes, now we're putting them in. We're allowing it. We're encouraging pilots to get trained.

It took me four months to convince the front office and the people involved in the training program in Georgia that we could develop a session with the national media to give them some sense for what we were doing. We had to scrub the curriculum. We had to work with the participants in that first class of pilots—for everyone wanted to see the first class of pilots who volunteered. Then ultimately, I had to deliver. I had to show them through the coverage, which is a little scary, because you don't control what the media does. I had to show the people who I had talked into doing this, that we could do it without giving anything away.

So, you put a little bit of your credibility on the line. You go in and you say, "I can get this done, but you have to let me do it the way I tell you to do it. I will work with you. If there's something that you think Osama Bin Laden is going to use against us, you tell me. We'll find a way to get that out of the program, but in the end, we have to give them something. We can't leave them all at the front gate."

It was a long process, and thankfully, I had great staff around me. We worked hard on it. We went to Georgia a few times to sit down and walk through it all before the nation's and the world's media showed up at the door to see this. We organized it, we managed it very tightly, and in the end, the coverage was awesome.

We created a program that I think they still use to some extent to this day. That training is to some degree open to the media. Not all of it, there are some tactics that we don't want any adversaries to know about because that would help them find a way to breach the cockpit, but there are some things you can show that aren't going to give anything away. We found a way to split that issue right down the middle. We walked a tightrope from Day 1 to the end, but we delivered it.

One challenge we faced is how do you simplify complex information. It's different with every situation. It was easy in that case because the people we were working with who were not communicators didn't want to give the media anything. They just wanted to say no comment to everything. When I took over that office, that's what they were doing, and they were wondering why their media program was so bad. The media was attacking them all day long because they had nothing to eat. They were hungry, nobody was giving them anything. We rolled out everything during that time. We were adding 5,000 screeners to the payroll every week. We were adding dozens and dozens of airports to the program every week. We were rolling out 100 percent checked bags. For people who are old enough to remember those days, the bags weren't being checked before that.

And then, we had to put in a program that ruined the award-winning airport lobbies that made them angry and slowed down the boarding process and caused everybody to have to leave their pocketknife at home. The whole thing made everyone upset despite what we saw on TV live on 9/11.

We just went through very calmly and tried to find ways to tell good stories. We knew that we were going to have to prove ourselves over and over and over again. We took baby steps. We didn't try to do the big stuff first. Guns in the cockpit was not until much later in our program.

It was a little easier than if that were the first thing we would do. If you're trying to get people in your organization to come along with you, to help you tell stories that can benefit your audiences and your organization, I would say start small. Get some credibility or bolster what you already have, and just do it by proving it. Over time, as people start to trust you more, it will be easier for you to do what you need to do when it gets tough.

Communicators know they need to be honest and accurate, but **Jay Baer**, bestselling marketing and CX author and inspirational speaker, highlights restaurants' ethical dilemma: COVID-19 disclosure:

I live in Bloomington, Indiana, a college town about an hour south of Indianapolis. Many of my friends here are in the restaurant business. It's a relatively small community. There's probably a hundred thousand people here all in, relatively close knit. What's interesting is when workers at restaurant A are diagnosed with COVID-19, which happens with some regularity because the restaurant community tends to congregate off hours. That being the case, restaurant A has a worker that has been diagnosed positive, sends that worker home and presumably quarantines them until they pass a negative test and then welcomes them back.

But in the interim, it's business as usual. That's option A. Option B, which happens some of the time, is the restaurant discovers that a worker has been tested positive, closes the restaurant for deep cleaning, tests all of the staff, and then publicly notifies the entire community. That is the exact same situation with an entirely different approach. It is a huge fork in the road.

I find it fascinating because it's literally playing out right in front of me every day in my community. Every day, another restaurant closes. Every day, another restaurant has a positive case, but doesn't mention it as reported. You find out usually anonymously on Reddit or somewhere like, "Yeah, somebody in the kitchen has it, they just didn't close." And it's interesting to see how the community reacts to each of those decisions.

Those who are aware of businesses hiding positive tests are unhappy and threaten to not spend money in those businesses for the foreseeable future. The challenge is that the people who stay up on those kind of things on a Reddit is a very small minority of the overall population. It's going to filter out via word of mouth in a town like this eventually, but it's not the same as making an announcement on your Facebook page or in your e-mail, or even on the homepage of your website that, "Yes, indeed, we had a positive test and we closed as a result for three days to make sure everybody else tested negative." I find that to be an interesting ethical conundrum.

What's been heartwarming is that where restaurants have proactively said, "We have to stay closed for a few days and retest everybody." The community has rallied behind that in an unbelievable way.

That kind of reaction is heartwarming, but by the same token, nearly every restaurant is struggling at almost an existential level right now. While the ethical decision to keep quiet is perhaps puzzling on the surface, you understand why when the question is "If we have to close, are we even going to be able to reopen?"

When you are caught in wrongdoing, how much do you need to say?
José Manuel Velasco, Past President of the Global Alliance for Public

Relations, shares what he did when the company he worked for was caught making illegal payments:

> The most difficult challenge I faced was the publication of the so-called Bárcenas papers in Spain. It was a case of illegal financing of the popular Conservative Party in Spain.
>
> The company for which I was working then appeared in those papers. They conducted an internal investigation, and we recognized that the company had actually made payments to this illegal network. We were the only company in the sector that recognized the payments, although they did not coincide with the notes that appeared on the papers. It was different payments. But we did pay to this illegal network.
>
> All other companies that appeared in the papers denied the payments or shut up. It was very difficult to convince the top management to do something different from the competitors and speak up. In my opinion, many companies are going to be in trouble because of their behavior.
>
> We spoke up because the best communication strategy is truth. The papers were a very deep investigation about the relationships between many construction companies and marketing companies that were also working for the Conservative Party. There was a strong link between the payments of the construction companies and the events that the party was organizing. In theory, they were paying with this illegal money.
>
> The decision was between following ethical or the legal advice. The legal view was very restrictive. The main goal was to protect the company. I also wanted to protect the company, but I thought we'd have to tell the truth because sooner than later, the truth will appear.
>
> It was very helpful that the CEO of the company was appointed recently, and it was an issue from the previous administration. He was convinced that he had to make a strong decision.
>
> For the company, thinking internally, it was a very good opportunity to make a strong decision about ethics, because the decision made by the CEO telling the truth that we have to make some payments to this network, was unusual. He used the opportunity

to change the mindset of the company and to show that we have to keep different values.

Looking back, I would have changed many things. But as the Frank Sinatra song says, "I don't regret anything." I don't regret anything not because I don't have things that I could regret, because I have several, but because it's not worth punishing yourself for something that happened in the past and you cannot change. You cannot change the past, but you can change the way you act. In my opinion, you have to learn from mistakes. That is very important, to recognize that you have made some mistakes in the past. It's a very good opportunity to learn from mistakes, from failures, including bad things.

Michelle Egan, APR, Fellow PRSA, Chief Communications Officer of the Alyeska Pipeline Service Company, faced another horrifying issue when the company for which she works, equipment caused the death of a middle schooler.

The company that I work for has a lot of heavy equipment and trucks out on the road. One afternoon I was in my office and a vice president came in and said, "I'm going to need your attention right away. This is not a good situation."

A large truck had been involved in an accident with a bicyclist, a middle-school student on his way home from school. The student didn't survive the accident. It was a very sad and extremely unusual type of event to happen in our organization because of our safety focus.

The accident wasn't the driver's fault. It wasn't due to any equipment malfunction. But on the day of the accident, we did not know that. Just like any other crisis, you know very little about the facts.

We have what we call a "no surprises" approach to communication here, that's our strategy. It means that we immediately go out with information to the appropriate stakeholders as soon as we know something. We notified our employees right away of the incident and our stakeholders, and I responded to media inquiries.

Then, of course, an investigation was launched immediately by law enforcement, and we participated. That is consistent with our company values around truth and transparency. Also that day, our senior leadership gathered to talk about what actions should be taken, keeping records, cooperating with the investigation, reaching out to the contractor—for it was actually a contractor of ours that was driving the vehicle.

In this meeting, I recommended that our president make contact with the mother of this young boy who died. The recommendation wasn't about public relations. I had no intention of sharing with anyone that this call was made, but it felt like the right thing to do in terms of the compassion that we want to show for the people that we impact. That was my recommendation, but for many good reasons, other executives counseled against any contact at that time. They had lots of good and legitimate reasons, and I wasn't sure that what I was suggesting was the right thing to do other than it felt like the right thing to do. I wasn't sure if making the phone call was the right thing to do in terms of what was best for the company, but it just felt right.

Everyone else on the executive team thought this wasn't the right thing to do. They had a lot of good reasons. Reasons like, we don't know the facts of what happened. We don't want to interfere with the investigation. We might be facing a lawsuit and we don't know what that will be about. Probably most importantly, we don't know if this is a sensitive or an insensitive thing to do. We don't know how this mother will take it. Everyone's experience of grief and shock is different. And so, for about 48 hours, I talked to each of the execs and got their opinions, and our president still was unsure whether he wanted to do this or not.

But he had a long career in the military, he'd had many occasions to reach out to people who'd lost someone. He's a kind and thoughtful man. Talking to the mother was consistent with who he is and consistent with our company and our values.

In the end, I worked with all of our executives to find a way that he could make this call. He wanted to reach out to this woman. We worked together, and we agreed that I would sit in on the call, that it would be brief. We agreed on what he would say and also that I would take notes so that we would have a record of this call. It was a real privilege to be included in that.

We compromised and found a solution everyone was comfortable with, and in the end, it was the right thing to do.

One important thing for practitioners to know is the people that we work with all bring an important perspective to the table. There were a lot of perspectives that needed to be considered. It was a difficult phone call because of the pain the mother was in, but mostly the call was just listening to her talk about her son. And it felt like we had been the compassionate organization that I know we are.

When you counsel a senior leader, you have the trust of that individual—you get to see them in some pretty, pretty raw times. It's quite a privilege.

There's some work by Dr. Marlene Neill that's very powerful where she looked at senior practitioners and how they navigated ethical issues. One of the strategies that she found that practitioners are using most often is building alliances. This was an example where the alliances that I had built over many years came into play.

I use them all the time, because again, we don't always have the best answers or the best solutions. I've been lucky to work with some people in our legal department who have a great perspective. We say, "Let's talk about what you want to do, what you think we should do, and then let's find the way to do it that all of our risks are going to be considered, not just reputation risk."

Ken Hunter, President and Chief Strategist at The PowerStation, faced disclosure issues when one of his clients was accused of making people sick.

I had an organ and tissue procurement organization for transplants as a client. This company specialized in bone tissue. All of a sudden, they were running into cases where patients were contracting hepatitis, and they weren't sure if it was from them or the hospital. The FDA came in. The CEO was in a very big panic wondering, what should I do about this? They may shut us down. Our reputation is going to be ruined.

As a PR person, you have to try to balance the potential of lawsuits versus the public's right to know, versus are we going to just create broad panic for no reason at all? We haven't yet confirmed what the problem was. It took a couple of months to finally find where the problem lay. It was something where the testing wasn't even picking up the fact that there was hepatitis in some of the bone tissue that they would give to hospitals to transplant into people.

By the time that happened, there were lots of stories in the press and the big warning about doing business with this company. They suffered a big blow to their reputation for a while but were able to bounce back.

We counseled them to be honest, to tell here's what we know now versus speculation. That helped us bridge the ethical gap. We had to decide between baring our souls or being a little more measured in what we put out and wait until we know for sure that X has happened before we go and tell everybody X has happened. That approach worked well. I know the FDA, when they were finished with their investigation, was happy in how the company was transparent.

During that case, I learned a fair amount about how to handle openness without saying, okay, everybody, here, come take a look. Pry through every file we've got. Taking a measured approach ends up serving the public better.

If others find themselves in a similar situation, first of all, you must build trust with the CEO and top management team. In this case, it included physicians, who weren't necessarily skilled in communication techniques. The executives recognizing it is a serious situation that's going to involve more expertise than just medical was big positive. Get trust by winning a couple of small battles in the beginning. From that point, start to work down from the CEO. Because now that the CEO trusts you, the medical director will tend to start trusting you more and other executives, the head of sales, you name it, will trust you. It'll trickle down from the top.

At companies, the whole personality of the place comes down from the top. In this case, it was very good that the CEO was very open with his team, letting them know he didn't have all the answers but is trying to protect this place.

I can remember another time dealing with a hospital system who was in the middle of a possible nurses strike. We're in the war room, and I'm sitting across as outside counsel. The attorney and I are going back and forth. The attorney is worried about how big the lawsuits will be or how bad will we get burned in negotiations. The CEO was perplexed and started to develop a very personal dislike for the union side, for their negotiators who also had a personal dislike for the hospital side.

At one point; I was letting everybody vent and telling the lawyer this is going to be a long-term reputational problem that we need to think about. I remember the CEO just looked at the lawyer, looked over at me and said, you know something, I'm glad that we have PR here because I wouldn't even have thought of these things. It got to the point where it was so hateful between the people involved because they were just so personally connected to it. They were very happy to just tell somebody else, here, I'm going to vent my spleen. I'm going to tell you everything that's driving me nuts. It ended up working well, and they were able to get through that. A lot of times I will see top execs have taken things so personally by the time they have a communication person come on into the picture, it's to their detriment.

To help executives get beyond feeling they are being attacked personally, I usually will let them vent in the beginning. It's very important that people have that opportunity to tell their side of the story. Even though I may be *paid* by that CEO to come on in to help that person, I still try to be more of an impartial jury. Because I don't have those years of experience in that company leading up to whatever that situation is, to see if the company culture potentially permitted this, or is there just a failure of an individual employee?

I like to serve as a quasi-devil's advocate and go through who the different target audiences are for that company or issue. That helps them see the impact of whatever the decision is that's made and are we including everybody. Do we have employees as a group that may be impacted? When you start running through the different target audiences, that tends to be an eye-opener because people usually naturally go to our customers as the start and the finish of the target audiences. That is a mistake.

Loring Barnes, APR, Fellow, PRSA, discusses tough ethical issues with disclosure of information in product recalls:

I was involved in a fairly famous product recall fail involving a tent that was manufactured by a very respected European outdoor product manufacturer. They had come to the United States, and we had just guided the company's most successful national consumer product campaign, which was PR driven with very light, but creative advertising support. The advertising agency had launched 10-second ads that underscored the value proposition of this tent, which was that you literally threw it up in the air, and it unfolded.

When the ad tells you that next we will invent instant campfire—you are not expecting somebody from within the organization to come to you and say, "You know what? We've just discovered that this tent has not satisfied the more stringent fire-retardant standards of the USA. It had passed lesser standards overseas, but not in the US."

I am the person who stood forward to the then U.S. CEO and said, "We need to act. We need to stop the work that we're doing, and we need to do a 180 and we need to get these tents back." Because not taking decisive and ethical action would have left families and children potentially at risk because where do you use a tent? You use it when you're camping. And probably you have a campfire nearby. This was a potential disaster.

The CEO did not want to stop the campaign because he knew it was terrifically successful. Our work had paid dividends. There was a very high return on the campaign investment and very high response by consumers across the country for a brand that had very little national footing at that time. I pulled the plug on the campaign. I said, "You know what, I'm sorry but this is not only your corporate reputation, but this is my reputation and that of my team and it is wrong to continue to do this." We ended up going to Europe and explained to the corporate leadership there why it was that we felt that this was the action to take.

At the end of the day, they recognized the ethical decision that we had put before them, and they released the U.S. CEO. We proceeded with a product recall with the consumer product safety commission. We did the right thing.

If other people find themselves in similar situations, this is where the Internet is your friend. It is not hard to find a story that has a parallel track of a problem that you could indicate to be transferable and instructive. You can say, "This is not a new road, here are the consequences that these other organizations suffered." When you can show the true revenue cost and impact from doing the wrong thing, you're going to have some stronger footing for showing them that redemptive action is always the way to go.

There's no shortage, sadly, of stories where individuals', leaders', and brands' reputations have eroded when they have done the wrong thing. You can easily point to them and say, "Do you want to travel this path? If not, these are the steps that we need to take. And I have the professional training and confidence and department to guide you through this. I understand that an organization is not just the people from within, it's all these other stakeholders and that the messaging and the activities that you need to take are very different."

Walk the talk. Bad behavior never happens privately. It happens in public. We all have a cell phone. We're all whistleblowers. An organization doesn't own its ethical reputation. It has to live an ethical reputation, but the referendum on how they do and how they behave against an expected moral compass happens well outside of the corner office, and that's how any organization recruits and retains talent, which foremost are the most effective and credible. Without that understanding, you're missing a major gap in the lifeblood of any organization's growth and success.

Disclosure of information hit close to home for **Kelli Bravo**, VP Healthcare, Pegasystems. She had to address the ethical considerations in admitting an error in their software.

A while back, I worked at a healthcare IT company that also provided healthcare content. One year, one of our software content releases had a major error. Not just a typo, but one that affected the workflow. The dilemma was centered around what to do next. Do we re-release the product, which costs a lot of time and money, or do we just communicate about the error and hope folks catch it when they use the content?

Back then, software releases followed a waterfall approach, which meant it could be a three- to six-month release cycle because it wasn't just a patch. You needed a full QA process. You had to reissue the software, retrain the clients on how it is used, and how it worked, which was time consuming and expensive.

We sat back and we said, what should we do now? We conferred with our software team, the content developers, and a bunch of our clients to determine the best path forward. We knew it was expensive. It was going to be time consuming to reissue this software. But at the end of the day, it was the right decision.

We ultimately moved forward with a new release, but it took a lot of conversation. This new release required a reissue, new client training, and admitting the fact that we had made a mistake. In today's agile, low-code/no-code environment, this process would have had a much lower cost and more rapid turnaround, a lower client impact. It would have made the decision a whole lot easier, but ultimately, I think we would have absolutely come to the same conclusion. You have to do the right thing.

To make this happen, we discussed the tradeoffs and being able to tell the organization that at the end of the day, we all want to work for an organization that acknowledges its mistakes. Because your reputation and the reputation of your company holds fast when you do the right thing. The right thing includes admitting when you make a mistake. As long as you learn from that, it's okay. It shows that you and your company are mature, accountable, and care about your customers. Lay it out and show the financial impact, the reputation impact, client and employee feedback.

At the end of the day, people do business with organizations and other people they trust. If they were to find out that we hadn't been trustworthy, we would have lost more than we would have gained from the financial impact. It's a long-term play. If you can't continue to maintain trust with your customer base, you will not continue to grow and succeed. The right decision comes forth as a result of putting your thinking cap on and having that collaborative discussion with your executives to help them understand and frame the problem.

Hiding something in a bullet on page 98 isn't going to be the process that works for me or my team. Be very direct and clear. Recognize people don't typically hear the message the first time. You need to share it two or three times to ensure that people understand the difference.

Don't be swayed from your convictions by things like cost or convenience when it is the right thing to do. It's okay to make a mistake, but you need to be accountable for it and show that you care about your customers.

Time Pressure and Disclosure of Information

BJ Whitman, APR, Fellow PRSA, a PR professional, faced an ethical issue with timely disclosure of information when it came to the death of an employee.

It was a regular day for me at work. I was on my way down to meet the executive chef at 9:00 a.m., and I got a call from the executive office saying, "Hurry to the kitchen. There is something wrong with the chef." I walked into a kitchen in complete chaos. Employees were crying, some people were running out of the kitchen, and a couple of the employees were holding an employee who had just stabbed the chef, who was on the floor in a very bad condition. A number of employees were kneeling down beside him trying to comfort him.

I immediately called 911 and called the executive office to let them know that the ambulance was on the way. I knew the chef had a brother who worked at a hotel nearby, so I called him and let him know what hospital to go to. The general manager was not at the hotel, he was on the mainland, attending his own father's funeral. So, the assistant manager and I oversaw the crisis.

At 11:00 a.m., the employees were told that the chef died from the injuries received from the stabbing, and immediately the media frenzy began. It was a hotel of 1,000 employees, who are in complete mourning over this wonderful beloved chef. He was a wonderful person, who was personable and dedicated to all of his employees.

By noon, we provided background information to all the media through a press conference, and those at the hotel who had e-mails. The only item I could not get to the media right away was a photograph of the chef. We had sent three photographs to the family to choose from that we had on record. The picture finally was chosen by 3:00 p.m., and released to the media, in time for the evening news and for the following morning daily papers.

But during that timeframe, I had received harassing and unprofessional calls, e-mails, messages, and even scoldings in front of other reporters from one TV reporter. But it was worth the wait for the family. It was a picture that ended up living on for many years.

Whenever there was another incident in the hotel or a violent incident in any hotel in Waikiki, the chef's picture was used. Unfortunately, the chef's family had additional tragedies when the son fell off a cliff and died. Again, the chef picture was used. So, in a very, very odd way, I was proud that we had the patience and the wherewithal to wait and didn't force the family to pick a picture that they wouldn't have otherwise been happy with.

I considered the behavior of the TV reporter unethical, and certainly, there was no cause for the nastiness and belligerence that she had presented. The sentiment is supported by the rest of the media who were considerate about the fact that the family wanted time to choose a picture that they could actually accept.

My advice to others is build things like family approval into your process. And you have to be willing to tell reporters that they will get it, but they will get it upon the approval of the family.

Mike McDougall, APR, Fellow PRSA, President of McDougall Communications, had a disclosure issue when clients made up news.

I had a client who on their own they went out and announced that they had an employee relief fund around a natural disaster that had just struck.

They wanted to be in the global conversation around this natural disaster and to be seen as forward looking and helpful of their employees. The challenge was twofold. One, there were very few employees of the company in the area where this natural disaster occurred. So even if there was a relief fund, it was great but would have minimal impact. Two, there was no employee relief fund. They purely generated this for the media exposure.

It came to my attention about two hours later. Unfortunately, I was traveling. It was an issue that happened in Asia during the overnight hours and early morning hours when I was still asleep on the West Coast. I woke to a series of e-mails and texts from peers asking about this employee relief fund. Why hadn't they heard of it?

We quickly advised the CEO of the company that we should retract this. Remove it and apologize that it was put out, not even in error, but put out without proper counsel and then stuff the genie back in the bottle as much as we could. Unfortunately, the person who drove this doubled down and so much wanted to be part of the conversation. They continued to make contacts on their own. We found ourselves facing questions from media later that day for details around our employee relief fund. How long had it been in existence? What do you plan to do? We chose to be honest to the extent we could with media by saying that those details were not available. We needed to evaluate how this would be operationalized without throwing the organization under the bus. And then we pushed for and got the establishment of an employee relief fund immediately. If we're going to say we have one and we don't, we'd better create one now.

Oddly enough, the view inside the organization and particularly the executive who was pushing this was, "No, we don't need to. We can just say we have one. We'll figure it out later."

That's probably the most egregious ethical breach I've seen in my career. Honestly, he thought he was smarter than anyone else in the world and no one would figure this out.

My view of crisis communications is don't put your brand in front of a crisis knowingly. A natural disaster's not a place I want my brand to be. Unless there's good reason for it to be there. That was a horrible, horrible situation. We mitigated it.

There are times when you can get involved. When I was working for Bausch & Lomb, we would ship an 18-wheeler full of eye drops and solutions to the firefighters working the California wildfires. Why? Because it's the right thing to do.

Sure, we told our industry that we were doing this. But we didn't hype it. We made them aware because others were doing the same thing. It was being part of a community that ultimately was looking out for our customers and looking out for the country. That's the right thing to do. That's going to come back and help you. Shameless promotion is not. People see through that pretty quickly.

Dianne Danowski Smith, APR, Fellow PRSA, President and Founder of Publix Northwest, shares her insight into how to deal with unreasonable reporters seeking disclosure in unethical ways.

I received a call at 2:45 from a reporter writing on a very controversial story. The reporter was making statements that just make you cringe. And by the way, the reporter's going to file the story at 3:00, and do we have a comment?

I always interview a reporter before I let them interview my client. I want to make sure that the reporter is as informed as possible. Sometimes the reporter's going to need some background.

This reporter was known to be a difficult reporter to work with. I pushed back on the reporter. I said, "Well, it sounds like you've got the story already written by the questions you're asking me." And I said, "You're filing it at 3:00 and it's 2:48 right now." I said, "Does that seem fair to you since your story is about my client's company?" I actually said, "Is that ethical? You're not giving us a fair opportunity to rebut your accusations or to provide information that might take your story in a different direction."

The reporter did not appreciate me saying that.

I said, "Well, I'm going to work my hardest to try to get the information. Our chief medical officer would be the perfect person. They're very familiar with this situation." But the chief medical officer wasn't available before 3:00. I had to say, "If you can wait so I can get you an interview so you have a fair and balanced story, then I can get you with that particular professional." But the reporter didn't wait. He filed the story, and it was biased.

I tried going back to the reporter. The reporter wouldn't take my follow-up phone call when the story was published. I went to the editor at that point. And I said, "There's a very serious issue going on here." The editor didn't necessarily agree with me because I was a PR person and I asked about their policy on fairness, fair, and balanced coverage.

It ended up to being a good conversation or with the editor. A couple days went by, and I called the reporter again, and he took my call and he and I ended up having a very good conversation.

Industries can present their own disclosure of information issues. **David Calusdian**, President of Sharon Merrill Associates, shares insight with regard to investor relations.

In IR, you need to be honest about a company's performance. That's what it comes down to. It's an ethical issue, but it's also a legal one. The SEC will point out when you're being misleading by just focusing on the positives of a company's performance. What you said in a press release headline might be true, but if you aren't giving investors all the information they need to make an intelligent investment decision, then the SEC has an issue with that. Any good IRO will have an issue with that too. You need to communicate the good with the bad. It has to be holistic communication that in the end gives an investor all the information they need to make an intelligent investment decision.

You want to put your best foot forward, but most importantly, you have to be honest in what your overall communication is telling investors. That's where ethical issues occur. You may get pressured to only put the positive forward, but as a good IRO, you need to tell the whole story.

One of the trickiest issues deals with timeliness. Timing and disclosure are always connected. For example, companies are sometimes debating whether to pre-release poor performance before quarterly earnings, but they may not know how bad it's going to be. They may not know exactly if they're going to miss and by how much on a certain date, but they may want to give investors the heads up. So, they are then faced with the situation of do we go out right now and give incomplete information or do we wait a few days and make sure that we understand exactly where we're going to come in. Or wait until we have a reasonable assumption of where we're coming in and be able to discuss more of the factors that are going into that. There's that decision as to whether you wait and give better information or go out quickly.

There is no hard and fast rule. It's all situational. It's like a crisis. Sometimes a crisis will hit a company and you may not know all the facts, and the playbook may say, get it out as quickly as possible. But if you might know more information in the next day, you might want to give yourself the day. It's very situational, very company specific.

It's very easy to say get the information out as soon as you know it, but it's not always that easy. Sometimes you may get more information in the next minute, hour, or day that can help the public better understand the situation.

Ethical Disclosure of Information Advice

Influencers

Influencers are a powerful tool in a communicator's toolbox. Over the years, there have been hundreds, if not thousands, of ethical issues in dealing with them and disclosure of information. **Troy Brown**, President of One50one, shares his experience:

> Influencer marketing is riddled with ethical issues.
>
> I'm talking to brands now that still don't understand the notion of how to post or how to ensure that FTC guidelines are followed or how to engage. Those are table stakes.
>
> I won't out folks, but there are celebrity-level entrepreneurs that are hundred millionaires, billionaires. I dealt with a lot of those folks in the media entertainment industry, and they are spirit brand owners, they're clothing brand owners. These folks have brilliant minds. But you go to these people and say, "Listen, you can't run that influencer program this way because these folks are your friends and you're going to pay them." Or "They have to post like this. They have to…"
>
> And they say, "No, forget all that. I'm so-and-so. This is what we're going to do." I tell them, "Listen, ethically, you can't do that. You can't pay them like that, or you can't do it."
>
> You've seen some of them get fined, but a lot of these businesses and companies at this point will just take the fines because they want to do it their way.

Gary McCormick, APR, Fellow PRSA, highlights another issue professionals face:

> One disclosure concern I have deals with social media and public relations persons being active on their own channels. I've long asked the question about how effective a counselor or a public relations professional can be for their clients when they've already established their own social media personality with deliberate political or social views or opinions. I just question (and this is,

again, my personal opinion) but are you able to be equitable and balanced in your work for clients when you already have a pronounced opinion?

When you use your own social media and become a voice in a certain area, it will limit the clients that you can be a strong advocate for, and your own ability to see alternate views and opinions in counseling the client. We need to be very careful about our own channel and how much voice we put into that. All of us like a lot of things, and it's very easy to see a person's personality, opinions, and beliefs. There's a fine line between being more of an advocate and less of a counselor.

I say this much more to younger professionals. Social media channels are a natural thing to them, and I'm not sure they understand how very easy it is to evaluate by clients.

You need to think it through. If, ethically, you're fine with putting that out there and know it's going to limit you professionally or personally, I say go for it. But we need to just stop for a moment and ask how well can you represent your client?

Martin Waxman, APR, shares his experience with third-party influencers and disclosure:

I was working with someone who wasn't as transparent as I thought she should be. We had hired a third-party expert to do some interviews on behalf of our client. One of the tips they would mention was to use our client's product.

This manager thought we should send out the media advisory, but she wanted to do it without letterhead, on plain white paper, to book this person with no mention of the agency or the client.

I said, "That's wrong. You gotta be transparent. You gotta at least say, 'Presented by this person.'"

We had a big argument, but she was a senior person on the account, she won out. She wasn't able to accompany this person on the interview, so I was stuck taking this expert around. We got to one TV station, and I knew the producer quite well. The guy is unpacking his bag and he takes out one product, then he takes out another product, then he takes out another product. The producer came over to me and said, "Hey, what's going on here? We thought this was going to be about the book and there's all this product."

I said, "Well, I've known for you a long time and here's what the story is." She was so mad. She yelled at me for a long, long time. Rightfully so. I took the heat for that, and the agency was banned from the program for about a year or so. Rightfully so.

I was able to come back and make a case to say, "Hey, we can never do this again. It hurts our credibility, not being transparent, and what are we hiding? Why don't we be upfront? If they don't want to cover, they don't have to. We can move on and be creative."

When working with a third-party influencer, you must disclose. The FTC demands it. In Canada, they have advertising standards:

It's kind of is simple: don't lie, tell people who you are and who you represent.

That's one of the greatest things about social media. It's underscored the need for transparency and, in a way, has helped communications people step out of the shadows and not necessarily be perceived to be puppet masters who are pulling the strings

Tami Nealy, Vice President of Communications and Talent Relations for Find Your Influence, also shares her expertise with ethics and influencer relations:

You need to be open and honest about what you want, what you're looking for, what you want the content to be shaped like. And then you have to step back and empower the influencers to create that content.

The good news is in November of 2019, the Federal Trade Commission issued social media disclosures 101,[1] which is a

---

[1] Federal Trade Commission. November 05, 2019. "FTC Releases Advertising Disclosures Guidance for Online Influencers."

guide for influencers on how to disclose that the content that they are posting is either paid, so they were paid to post it, or whether it was gifted to them. Either way, they want to see that you're disclosing it with #ad or #sponsored or on Instagram you can tag the partner. You can say in partnership with X brand. You need to disclose that to your followers so that they understand that there was some level of compensation or gifting in exchange for that product. Most often the content and the experience that they had with it is authentic, but disclosing it is very, very, very important.

Other Advice

There are specific ethics issues in disclosure of information in security public relations. **Bryan Scanlon**, the CEO, Look Left Marketing, explains:

There's an absolute arms race going on, where it's the bad guys versus the good guys, and the bad guys are well-armed and very intelligent. And they're winning in some fronts. When an arms race happens, the rhetoric gets high.

What we're seeing in security now is some companies making some very big claims like, "We will stop all breaches." Or "We make breaches irrelevant." I find that language extremely disturbing. For me, it's like saying, "We have a car safety collision system and you'll never have a crash." Well, you could disable that and still have a crash. You could have somebody just back into you and have a crash.

That is creating these dangerous statements. There are so many vendors in security now. An average enterprise has 80 or 90 different tools. They all sound like they do the same thing, and in a high-stakes, risky environment where critical infrastructure could go down, or money gets stolen or medical devices could be hacked. There's a lot of room for hype there. The market's very crowded, so it forces you to one-up your competitor. When you put those things together, you get this hype machine that keeps going higher and higher.

Things have to change, but there's this temptation every day to do the "The sky is falling. The sky is falling." People are getting very tired of it and the ultimate danger is we just become numb to it, and people stop listening to the important stuff.

The first question I ask is, "Let's talk about facts. You say you can stop all breaches. Has your system ever been breached? Or did every one of your customers not have a breach?" And the answer is, "Well, of course, no. But that was other technology that got breached." It creates this discussion of just how farcical those claims could be.

Then we ask, why are we doing this? What is the problem that we're trying to solve? What is the pain for the customer, and how do we target that?

In security, there's a lot of cooperation between the vendors despite all of this hype and rhetoric. Because they believe in one thing that there are some bad guys out there, and we need to stop them. There's a serve and protect component. If we can steer people toward that and remind them that that's the business that we're in, things work out okay.

There is an ethical process for reporting security issues. It is called "responsible disclosure" and is very common in the security industry. The good guys, the vast majority of companies, abide by it. If you found a flaw in a version of Windows, or in an Alexa device—responsible disclosure's tenets basically say this: I'm going to contact that company and tell them that I found that problem. And they're going to have a chance to fix it, or have a patch available, before I disclose that. So, when you go public, you're disclosing something that is likely already fixed or solved, or you're contributing to the education of everyone of what they need to do to download or patch.

It's something that we always ask our clients. Did you disclose this? Do they know? Is the patch going to be ready? Because there is pressure in that competitive environment to release that news quickly before some other researcher reveals it.

There are people who have done a big show of disclosing vulnerability without contacting the company, and I find that highly unethical. Those people, pretty quickly, get some shade cast on them. You never want to put a user at risk.

However, there is this other disturbing thing that's happening a little bit in that I'm seeing the arms race come into play. Where, as part of that responsible disclosure, you're inevitably telling other researchers, and those researchers then, themselves, face an ethical dilemma of when do they jump on it? I actually had an instance last year where we were doing pre-briefings before responsibly disclosing a bug in critical infrastructure. A reporter called another researcher, and that researcher quickly put some stuff together, hacked it, and then released it ahead of our deadline, and risked going ahead of the problem being fixed. That's not appropriate.

Ron Culp, APR, Fellow PRSA, Professional Director, Graduate PR and Advertising Program at DePaul University, has advice for companies countering disinformation:

So many people think making a response is enough. It's not, especially if your employees are reading it. Your employees are going to read and believe about 40 percent of what they see online. Some companies will say, "We responded online. We clarified. Everyone is fine." Meanwhile, there are pockets of the organization that are saying, "Did you see that online?" It's just like a telephone game. By the time it gets spread four or five times, it becomes a bigger issue than you ever imagined.

If something appears about you, you want to make sure that you assess it quickly as to how much into the organization has this story spread, and is it something that we need to say something further, either through our internal website, Internet, or however we're going to communicate to employees, so they know our point of view. Because if you don't correct it pretty broadly, there's going to be a degree of people who are going to believe the mistruth that was said.

A lot of people will pooh-pooh what happens on social platforms, but there has been a lot more attention to how omnipresent it is and how vital it is for prompt response. Make sure you cover all your bases, or the next thing you know, a large number of people are going to be believing the mistruth.

Garland Stansell, APR, Chief Communications Officer for Children's of Alabama, has great overall advice on the best approach to ethical disclosure of information:

> If you only do the bare minimum of what is required legally, it can create more problems down the road. By being forthright and transparent and saying, yes, this happened. Here's what we've done and here's what we are doing, that satisfies the media and the public. If you are not being transparent and forthright, it can make you look like you were trying to cover up or hide something.

Five Key Takeaways

How do we maintain the highest ethical standards in disclosure of information?

1. People really do appreciate the truth. It builds stronger relationships.
2. If a stakeholder requires the information to make an informed decision, it is your duty to give it to them.
3. Mistakes happen. Fix them quickly.
4. Always disclose partnerships and sponsorships.
5. Beware of surprise and delight campaigns built around a lie.

CHAPTER 11

Safeguarding Confidences

Safeguarding confidences can often put communication professionals in a difficult situation. Do you tell a friend if they are about to be laid off? What about when a reporter asks you something you are not ready to reveal?

The PRSA Code of Ethics states:

> **Safeguarding Confidences**: Client trust requires appropriate protection of confidential and private information.
>
> The Intent is to protect the privacy rights of clients, organizations, and individuals by safeguarding confidential information.
>
> Three guidelines include:
>
> A member shall: Safeguard the confidences and privacy rights of present, former, and prospective clients and employees.
>
> Protect privileged, confidential, or insider information gained from a client or organization.
>
> Immediately advise an appropriate authority if a member discovers that confidential information is being divulged by an employee of a client company or organization.

PRSA gives to examples of Improper Conduct Under This Provision:

- A member changes jobs, takes confidential information, and uses that information in the new position to the detriment of the former employer.
- A member intentionally leaks proprietary information to the detriment of some other party.

But there are so many more issues to examine.

Safeguarding Confidences in Action

This is one of my favorite examples of safeguarding confidences. I think it skirts the ethical line, but doesn't cross it, and even 40+ years later, **Kirk Hazlett**, APR, Fellow PRSA, Adjunct Professor of Communication at the University of Tampa, is still keeping the details secret.

I had an interesting encounter very early in my career that drove home the point of ethical awareness and fast thinking and how little things and seemingly innocent questions can get you into a fix.

I was the public affairs officer for the U.S. Army Intelligence School at Fort Devens in Massachusetts. As the name might suggest, we were pretty super-secret, chain link fences, frosted windows, armed guards, all that kind of stuff.

But our student soldiers lived and worked and shopped in the local communities and wore their uniforms off base like any good soldier would.

My phone rings one morning in 1979. It's the editor of the local newspaper. He's got a question, and it's still in my head 40 years later. "I understand that you have soldiers from country X going to your school. Is it true?" Simple enough. But I knew that if I answered it as asked, I'd be guilty of releasing classified information.

Kind of a no-brainer here. I can't do that. If I try to dodge the question, the editor is going to get his answer anyway. He'll know that I'm doing it. I'll still be accused of having released the information. To make matters even more interesting. I'm looking out my office window. I see a group of soldiers from country X walking across our parking lot.

Here's what I said to the editor, "I have never been told that we have soldiers from country X enrolled here."

This response was the absolute truth. I had never been told by anyone that we had soldiers, or students, from other countries. If the editor decided to go ahead with it, he had an evasive, but a truthful answer from the school's public affairs.

The good news is the editor decided not to go with the story because he knew he was getting into some deep water. He couldn't say that the public affairs officer refused to answer my question or didn't get back to him because I was literally on the phone talking to him.

But there are lessons to learn here. As a person responsible for an organization's public relations initiatives, I absolutely have to be aware of everything that my organization is involved in. I have to be able to communicate it in a way that will maintain my own professional credibility while protecting my organization's right to privacy.

Moving forward, I made sure that I knew what the dickens was going on inside the organization. I poked my nose into everything so that I would be able to give stories to the public that did highlight the good stuff that we were doing. That people would say yeah, they're not the guys that live behind the chain link fences. They are people who are out in our community and doing valuable things. It's a matter of thinking and planning ahead. In every organization I've worked with, I say what's going to happen here that I'm going to be the one that's going to have to answer the questions, so what do I need to know about this?

Know what it is that you're doing and be ready with the answer. You never know when you're going to get a question.

Helio Fred Garcia, President of Logos Consulting Group, shares how Goldman Sachs taught him why even in difficulty situations you need to think long term when safeguarding confidences:

One of the principles I teach my students and my clients is the old principle from the guy who headed Goldman Sachs in the 1980s. It's okay to be long-term greedy. It's not okay to be short-term greedy. It's a foundational ethical principle that if you organize yourself for sustainability in the long term, you will avoid taking short-term shortcuts that might be ethically suspect. If you want to be sustainable for the long term, you're not going to take short-term ethical shortcuts. Short-term greedy bad. Long-term greedy good.

When I'm talking to business leaders or when I'm talking to people who are the stewards of reputation, I sometimes use the word stakeholder, but I'd rather use the purely accessible term— those groups of people who matter to you. The CEO, your investors, your employees, the regulators, the customers. What are their trust drivers? We need to make decisions that are more likely to result in either maintaining or restoring trust. It's much harder to restore trust after it's been lost than it is to maintain trust in the first place. So, let's get it right the first time. Measure twice, cut once.

Mike Paul, President of Reputation Doctor, takes a contrary stance and believes personal relationships may be more important than safeguarding confidences. It all comes down to where you believe you have the strongest duty.

I left Hill & Knowlton to go work for a corporation that ended up eventually merging with MCI WorldCom. Long story short, I had found based on someone I was dating at the time that my boss and several other bosses were on a list to be laid off soon. Because she cared about me, she thought I was probably going to be in the list too. She's been told to draft this memo for executives of MCI, and she told me about it.

She was so freaked out about it, she said she didn't want to talk on the phone, she wanted to talk in person. I met her and she handed me this draft memo. I had an ethical dilemma to decide on the spot, "Do I do something with this thing I'm about to read, or am I only corporate loyal?" Well, the guy who had given me the job, had taken me from Hill & Knowlton and brought me into the telecom company, he was a great guy, and we had a good relationship. I trusted him and he trusted me. He even called me his consiglieri. I knew where he was. I knew I didn't want to just talk to him about it. I knew I had to be face to face with him because he was going to have to make some big decisions soon. Two weeks from that time, this was going to happen.

I simply said to her, "Can I have this?" She said, "This is just a draft." She said, "What are you going to do with that?" I said, "I'd rather not tell you, so you don't get in trouble." I took that draft copy, I jumped on the plane, and I went to see him.

That evening I had dinner with this person, and I simply said, "Read this, don't touch it." I held it up, so he didn't have to touch the paper, because I fully wanted to be the person who was involved in the decision. He freaked out, I said, "Read it again because it's not going to be here in a couple of minutes." He read. I went to the bathroom, flushed it down the toilet, came back, sat down for dinner. I looked him in the eye and said, "All right, what are we going to do now?"

He said, "Mike, you have no idea what you just did for me and my family. Three things. Number one, I've been offered a job to go back to a big four accounting firm. Two, I have to make a decision within a week whether I'm buying this second home." Three, he had to make a major decision regarding his kids that was going to be an expensive decision, "and I can delay this decision now based on what I now know." He ended by saying, "I'm taking that job."

Now, he and I had been on phone calls, almost a year before that that were for leaders within the company, and he wanted my gut feel on the verbiage that was used and the tone that was used by leaders of MCI WorldCom, really from the WorldCom side of the team, on those phone calls.

Part of my feedback to him and a bigger boss who came from the MCI world that was on that phone call was, "These guys sound like cowboys," I said to them both. "So, you want my gut feel of what I just heard, I didn't hear shareholder value, I didn't hear what our customer needs are. I heard, 'We're going to win.' It's like a Ponzi scheme call. They scared the hell out of me." They both looked at each other and said, "We felt the same way."

That was an important phone call for our own heads to start thinking about our futures. And then this happens.

He said, and this reminds me of the negotiations like all of the actors in *Friends* who decided, "It's all of us or none of us." He included me on that list with three other people, and basically said he's negotiating for us to get an equal package pro-rated based on what we're making now, with various things that he's asking for. Four days later, the negotiation was over, and we all moved on.

We then now know only months later what happened to WorldCom. People were literally walking out in handcuffs. But we were gone. We had an ethical dilemma as to what we were going to do based on things that we know. We chose and risked our own futures by saying, "Time to leave," but felt comfortable that it was the best decision for us.

When it comes to safeguarding confidences, my answer is very, very clear. What supersedes that is the values that you either have or you do have not that were learned when you were being brought up. When I'm dealing with very powerful men who are in their 60s, 70s, or 80s about fraud that they were involved in, I talk to them from a moral perspective. I know some of them were using other firms before they hired me, because they weren't getting good advice. Some of them say simply right to your face, "No one had the balls to tell me the truth." I said, "You got the right guy for that."

I've had people call me the N-word as I'm counseling them because of the fear that kicks in, literally, "You effing N." Two weeks later, I'm at the dinner with that same person and his wife, and his wife says, "He told me what happened … how are you here? I don't understand how you would forgive him."

I said, "Easily. I have prepared myself for a response of A, B, C, D or E, not just A. I am trained to think worst-case scenario. That's what you do in crisis management work. I know I could put myself in his shoes, not exactly, but with enough experience to go, "He just freaked out. He's now realizing what he's said. He's embarrassed to call me back. He knows I can help him, and I will help him. And he knows the other guys that are on the team want to spin and lie for him." That's what made him call back."

I had to tell that guy, "You're not going to be CEO again, but you can be an amazing coach and councilor, you can write a book." You could say, "It was gut-wrenching. I learned the wrong things growing up…" You could say all of it. You could let it all out, and you will help other people. He's one of the top coaches out there now.

While every industry has confidential information, the health care and financial services industries have even tighter guidelines. **Erica Sniad Morgenstern**, Chief Marketing Officer, Virgin Pulse, shares her insight into top ethics issues in health care:

A big topic in the healthcare industry right now is data and transparency. A lot of people are concerned about the privacy of their information, how it's being used, who's using it, where it's going. I'd say that would be in any aspect of your life, but with health care, it's so much more personal. It's a challenge for data-driven organizations to help educate people about why it's important that some of your data is used to serve you up better.

I'm willing to use Google Gmail for free, and they're collecting data so I might get a more relevant ad. So why can't that apply to health care? There are some valid concerns. For example, I don't want my company to know if I have X, Y, and Z. Because they might treat me differently. I totally understand that. I'm in the same boat as well, but to the same degree, there's machine learning. People aren't looking at the information, they're collecting the data and applying it to serve you better. Who doesn't want that?

There are two types of situations. Ancestry.com DNA, that's a one-to-one situation. They are matching you with your DNA data. Whereas, with a lot of other organizations, it's aggregated, encrypted, and encoded. It's not like all of a sudden my company is going to know that I have three kids and one of them has eczema. That's not information that they need to know, but my physician's office, they should know that.

Five Key Takeaways

How do we maintain the highest ethical standards when safeguarding confidences?

1. People do not trust people who share secrets.
2. Telling a reporter "I won't share that information" is fine as long as you give a reason why.
3. People are losing their privacy. Do what you can to preserve it.
4. Sit down and figure out which duties are most important to you.
5. Don't steal IP from your employer.

CHAPTER 12

Conflicts of Interest

Every PR professional will run into conflicts of interest. Some are straightforward and have clear guidance due to laws. Others are a bit murkier.

PRSA's Code of Ethics calls on all professionals to be cognizant in:

"Avoiding real, potential or perceived conflicts of interest builds the trust of clients, employers, and the publics."

The Intent is to earn trust and mutual respect with clients or employers, and to build trust with the public by avoiding or ending situations that put one's personal or professional interests in conflict with society's interests.

Guidelines include:

Act in the best interests of the client or employer, even subordinating the member's personal interests.

Avoid actions and circumstances that may appear to compromise good business judgment or create a conflict between personal and professional interests.

Disclose promptly any existing or potential conflict of interest to affected clients or organizations.

Encourage clients and customers to determine if a conflict exists after notifying all affected parties.

But sometimes, this is easier said than done. One of the most common issues deals with the knowledge pros gain throughout their career working at different companies or for different clients. Can they share nonconfidential information they gain while doing research for one company with another company a year later?

Ethics and Conflicts of Interest in Action

Jay Baer, author and motivational speaker, has advice on how to ethically work for competing companies.

I am confronted with ethical challenges all the time because we do content creation, influencer marketing, and joint thought leadership. For example, there is a business that is creating a new software package to allow their customers to communicate to the end user, using text messaging as opposed to e-mail or phone. The competitor that they're looking to disintermediate is already a partner of mine. I'm already doing a bunch of work with the other guys. This happens a lot because the world that I inhabit, I work every day with Salesforce and Oracle and Cisco and HubSpot. Almost everything I do every day has some sort of competitive stickiness.

It's not practical to offer a category exclusivity per se, but I am constantly having to tell people, "These other guys who may be your sworn enemy, also want to work with me in this capacity. How do you feel about that?" In almost every case, I could probably do it without telling anybody, it's a big world, they wouldn't even notice. But I feel driven by the golden rule in this perspective that if I was working with a vendor who was working with my number one competitor, how would I feel about that? I'd at least want to know. I spend a lot of my time giving people heads ups.

I say to myself and my team, if the client actually did hear about this not from us, but saw a LinkedIn ad that said, "Jay Baer's going to do a webinar with your primary competitor." how would we feel about that? How would we feel that they would feel? If it's at all less than delighted, then the instruction is, nobody should hear anything other than from us directly. On occasion, it absolutely positively costs us money. They say, "You know what, we're just not comfortable with it. Don't do it." Then we just don't do it. We walk away. I feel like, especially in this day and age, disclosure is critical. We do so many joint ventures. There are a lot of things on there that say sponsored. We just want to make sure that people know where the bread is buttered. I wish everybody kind of went at it the same way, but I can tell you firsthand, they don't.

An even trickier problem is not inadvertently reusing insight gained from one company with another. As a speaker, I deliver insights to tens of thousands of people a year. If those insights gained on any individual project had to be kept in a lock box, that would be a real challenge. So, I don't worry about that too much, unless it truly is something that is applicable solely to that company or that industry. What makes me an effective speaker, author, and communicator is the scenario where I'm working in a lot of industries and working with lots of different companies all the time and can identify patterns and create hybridized advice and counsel that suits a lot of situations and circumstances.

There's a lot of things that we have to forget, but then there's also particular practice groups or verticals that you work in more often. We do a fair bit in higher ed now. There's no question that what we learn working on one school, we try to make ourselves smarter and apply it to a different school. The nice thing is that for the most part, the competitive juices in higher ed are not quite the same as they are in, say, software. They don't have quite the same issues. Right now we work with Arizona State and Arizona, we work with Purdue and Indiana.

Michael Smart, a leading media relations trainer and coach, keeps it very simple—you should always choose ethics over revenue. Conflict of interest also deals with your personal values.

When I first started as a speaker and trainer, I was still working full time, and I would be excited every time somebody called and asked if I'd consider coming to train them. At the time, the amount of money I could make doing a training gig was about 1/10th of my annual salary. These were big opportunities. One day, a call came, and she outlined all the things she needed, and explained that their previous trainer had fallen through. She had her team coming from all around the world on this given day, and she had to have somebody. It was only a month away, and please, please was I available?

I said, "So far it's sounding good. Tell me about the types of news stories that you'd like to get more coverage about." She said, "Well, our primary lines of business are vodka and cigars."

That is funny, because my whole life, I've chosen not to drink alcohol or smoke. I make no value judgments about other people who do, but that's an important value to me. My wife and I raised our kids with that choice, and I immediately knew it'd be hypocritical if I went and coached people how to get more media coverage for something that I don't believe in.

I heard her out. I thanked her for interest. I told her it wasn't going to work for me. I made that decision on a value level, but it was also consistent with a utilitarian outcome, and that is I knew I would suck at training people in how to promote vodka and cigars.

When I watch *Jeopardy*, the potent potable category is horrible for me. I just don't know anything about alcohol. I believe that most of the time doing what most people would classify as the right thing is still going to help you end up better off in your career.

I missed out on that windfall payment, but I would have been uncomfortable the entire time if I'd taken that gig. I have a steady stream of new business inquiries from clients who are consistent with my values because I made that decision early on. So, I came out way ahead.

Ken Jacobs, ACC, CPC, an experienced consultant and certified coach, has a perspective on how to handle conflicts of interest.

When you're doing executive coaching, that's very one-on-one, helping the leader align their actions with their values. It's helping the leader remove energy blocks, things getting in the way of their success. As coaches, we believe that our clients have that wisdom within, have the knowledge with them. It is our job to work with them, to use a coaching methodology to ask empowering questions to get rid of what's getting in the way of that success. That's one of the big differences between coaching and consulting. Consulting, you're telling them what to do. With coaching, you're using empowering questions to light up their brain and help them remove what's getting in the way of that success and to figure out what would ultimately be the most fulfilling for them.

If there are two agencies, and even if they were top competitors and I'm helping the CEO or senior VP at one agency deal with their issues and get the most from their opportunities, the things they're dealing with can be very, very different than the ones at the agency next door. I'm helping them become more compelling leaders to increase the followership, to increase their influence. To me, that's not a conflict of interest.

I could be working with two competitive agencies on enhancing their profitability, but things getting in the way of their profitability might be very, very different things. For one, their expenses may be too high or not delivering value, for the other one, the ratio of salary and benefits is just out of whack. So, if I help both of them concurrently, it is not competitive.

The only possible time where I have a conflict, and it hasn't happened yet, is if I have two agencies who are highly competitive and if they were both wanting to hire me for business development. That hasn't happened yet, but the thing I grew up believing in the agency business was, it's about your current client. It's about the ones who have already selected you and honored you by hiring you and saying, "We want to work together." If I'm working with Agency A on business development and Agency B comes along and they're clearly competitors and Agency B says, "We'd like to work with you on business development." I turn it down without a thought, not even a heartbeat.

Because Agency A, we're already partners who are working together. I would refer Agency B to another consultant because if they want help, there's help out there. There's a lot of us out there, and I know the good ones.

One of the most common and significant challenges is where conflicting duties leads to conflicts of interest.

Philip Tate, APR, Fellow PRSA, shares his insight on practical transparency and conflict of interest:

> We recently were asked to author and op-ed piece for a local newspaper from a prominent businessman, who we didn't work for, but who knew us by reputation and is very well regarded in the community.
>
> Our client had hoped to have him support their position without revealing that he used to have a financial stake in the company. We insisted that his connection to the company, even if it was in the past, must be revealed as part of that op-ed. They pushed back on that a little bit, and we said, "That's a non-starter." I said, "And it can be as simple as Mr. Executive is currently the CEO of XYZ Company and is a former board member, or former investor, of ABC Company."
>
> I said, "You have to disclose that, otherwise it could be misinterpreted. It could be misconstrued and that would not be in your long-term best interest."
>
> Fortunately, the client took our counsel.

Balancing Duties

Kelley Chunn, Principal of Kelley Chunn and Associates, experienced this firsthand when her employer and her had diametrically different ideas:

> I've always kind of straddled the line between advocate and activist. I was a writer for one of the local network affiliates here in Boston back in the 1970s and my boss at the station was threatening to take a TV show geared toward the African American community off the air. And we did not have a lot of programs.
>
> There was a demonstration in front of the station. At the time, I didn't see it as an ethical dilemma. I'm going to go down and protest because I think the station should keep the program on

the air. I knew I was an employee, and I was taking a chance by demonstrating. It wasn't a huge demonstration. There were maybe 50, 75 people, some of whom were from the station and some of whom were from the community who were fighting to keep the show on the air. I went down to join the demonstration and then I went back upstairs to write about it.

My producer, who was an African American woman, read the story. I had written, "There are 500 people downstairs." She read the story and said, "Now, Kelley, you know there weren't 500 people downstairs demonstrating." So, I had to fix that.

Looking back on it, there were two issues. Is it a conflict? Nowadays some media don't even vote because they feel that it will be a conflict, even though it's a constitutional right. They don't want to take public sides about issues or candidates. In the media, one of your mandates is to be as objective as you can. I don't think anybody can be 100 percent objective, but you can be fair, and you can be a truth teller.

Clearly, there was an ethical issue, and some may say that there was also a conflict between working for the station and demonstrating against the policy of threatening to take the program off the air. The kicker is the program remained on the air and is on the air even to this day, although it has evolved so that it has more of a multicultural theme to reflect the demographics of today.

Mike Paul, President of Reputation Doctor, shares a chilling example of conflict of interest between loyalty to staff and your employer:

I worked for a major agency that had a lot of problems. They had sexual harassment suits, they had past racial issues. They had past ethical and illegal crisis of all kinds. A lot of lawsuits. They decided, at least in words, they wanted to change. One of the things that they wanted to change was to bring in some top corporate communications and crisis management help, and that's where I came in.

I had permission to hire a number of people fairly quickly. I hired six new people to come into the organization within a matter of weeks. They didn't know this agency that well. They knew me, and they were trusting in me to build the team to do some great things. All six of them happened to be women. All six of them happened to be at the top of their game and excellent at what they did. And all six of them also happened to be beautiful. I mention that because the crisis and the ethical violation that goes along with it deals with sexual harassment and sexual assault by some of my peers, senior executives with the agency.

Four of the women came to my office at the same time, some of them shaking, totally uncomfortable. I'm an expert in body language. I've been trained by former CIA and FBI operatives to understand body language. I can assure you, their body language at the time was not good. I knew something was seriously wrong. First thing that I said to them was, "Are you feeling unsafe on this floor right now?" And they shook their head yes. And I said, "In offices to the left of me?" And they said yes. "And in offices to the right of me?" They said yes. I said, "Okay." Now, I had a split second to make a decision, an important ethical decision. Am I now a steward of fiduciary responsibility in my job working for this corporation first, or do I listen to these amazing ladies who are suffering first? It's a big question.

I instantly said I'm on their side. I didn't take my business phone. I didn't take my business laptop. I took my personal iPad and my personal phone, and I told my assistant, "I'm going to be gone for a long two-hour lunch at minimum." I took them all, and I said, "If the other two are comfortable to come, I want to hear everything. I'm on your side." Now, you and I know that's what you're supposed to do ethically and morally, not under the guidelines of the corporation, under the guidelines of being a human being on earth.

But that's not how it usually goes. How it usually goes is someone might listen for a while, they'll take notes. They talk to HR. HR might say, "Gosh, how are we're going to handle this?" Further days go by, other senior executives above me get involved, and many times, nothing happens.

That was not going to happen this time. I had decided to use brinkmanship, a keyword when you're dealing with situations like this. I was willing to live and change my job based on what I heard. If it breached not just corporate guideline but moral decision-making, I'm out, and I'm going to make sure I take care of them the best I can. That's the decision I made when I took that phone and that laptop, and I went to lunch with them.

Their stories were horrific. They were not just sexually harassed but sexually assaulted. They had been there just a matter of weeks. My only prism that I listened to them through was, "What if this was my sister? What if this was my daughter?" That's the view that I had as I was listening. I told them after they were done telling me their horrific stories, "I am 100 percent behind you. I will be leaving here soon, and I will help you to get what you believe is a fair recourse for what you've been through."

I knew one of their fathers. He was a professional football player and he said to me, "Mike, you've helped me in the past with something. I trust you. I know you had nothing to do with this, but I'm telling you I know who touched my daughter. I'm still 6 ft 11, 320 pounds. Let him know I know where he lives."

I could assure you the conversations, the negotiations, and everything that went along with this from the start was not pretty on their side, the things they said, the lies that they were trying to coat these women with. I said, "I don't think you guys get it. Guess what I have access to. I have access to being a commentator and having relationships with global and national news for 28 years. They trust me. You think if I call them and tell them about the story that this is not going to impact both personal reputations and global brands and even stock price? I have no fear."

Do you know why I didn't have any fear? They don't control anything that I do.

I left my firm to try and help an organization change. I had a Plan B ready and was set to jump back to my firm before I started. I just shut down the website and had my freelancers doing their own thing. I could pick up the phone and say, "We're back, let's go." That's it. It's all it took to come back to business.

They're not used to that. They're used to people being afraid. They're used to people being fearful of not making money. They didn't have that this time.

Pam Campbell, APR, Fellow PRSA, the Director of Public Affairs at the Federal Reserve Bank of Kansas City, Oklahoma City Branch, shared a conflict of interest example with a nonprofit board:

I probably dealt with more behavior that I might consider unethical in my volunteer work. I don't know if that's because of a lack of training, or maybe because a lot of people volunteer for organizations for more reasons than just giving back. You're definitely there for networking. You're there for building relationships. Sometimes that leads to building business. But sometimes it leads to conflicts of interest.

Just to give a specific example, there's a volunteer, who is an executive at an events company. She would volunteer, work, and chair committees that hosted events. That makes sense. She's an expert at event planning and brings great value to that committee. Where the conflict of interest developed is that she would hire her own organization to do the work. She may offer the nonprofit a 10percent discount, but I never saw an effort to use it as a donation or maybe to search for another organization that would donate those services. I saw several examples of that practice.

There was also somebody who wanted to promote a nonprofit through a publication her organization produced, which sounds great. Please give us some promotion. I found out later that the nonprofit was billed for that media placement. That's something that never should have been agreed to.

It happens a lot of times. People compartmentalize their life. To stop this, boards should be open and honest in educating the board. Sometimes people have a firm hold on what business ethics is. They know conflict of interest is an absolute no. But then they don't think about it translating to other parts of their lives, to volunteer work. It's the same thing—no matter where you are, ethics still matter.

Dianne Danowski Smith, APR, Fellow PRSA, President and Founder of Publix Northwest, looks at a different conflict—between what is legally best and what is best for the public:

I woke up one morning and my client was on the front page of the newspaper, above the fold, for unethical and potentially illegal behavior. This client was working on a very high-profile public sector project for a large local city.

The newspaper story alleged my client was tucking away money to try to get cost overruns in the project approved without going through the proper channels as established by the city codes and the city compliance efforts. Technically, what my client had done was not illegal. It was done quite frequently in its business. The city council decided that the cost overruns for this project had hit a limit, and the city commissioner in charge of that bureau put a hard stop and said we've reached a budget limit. But my client and its partner still had a number of change orders that were being requested by the city that they had to execute. It looked like somebody was not going to get paid for the work that the city requested.

The partner came to my client and said, "This is going to be a cost overrun." And my client said, "Well, we'll pay you. And then we'll bill the city based on the change order," which is legal. The change order had been agreed to, but it was going to exceed the budget. What it looked like was my client was doing an end run around the city commission, and that's how the city hall reporter in the paper decided to play it.

I was shaking in my boots a little bit and I had to go back to the GM, and I say, "Okay, this might be a practice that you've engaged in before. But the perception of this practice is unethical. Whether it's legally okay, it doesn't look ethically okay." There was the perception that there was some back room dealing going on, and I said, "We have to figure out how you're going to handle this process going forward."

What we decided to do to call the city commissioner and say, "We saw today's paper. We want to let the public know that we've talked to you, and you tell us how you want to handle this. We want to make a public statement about how the city prefers to handle this." So, we made a joint public statement about it. The city was on board. The city didn't necessarily think we were being unethical, but that's still how it played out.

At first the executive wasn't on board, and he wasn't terribly happy with me that I was agreeing with a reporter. As PR people, we often play that very, very fine line. It's fine for a company to talk about transparency, but when you have to practice transparency, that becomes a very different conversation.

How did I get him on board? I told him, "I'm pretty nervous about having this conversation with you because I don't want you to walk away with a perception that I'm pointing the finger and that I'm making any accusation." But I said, "This perception is real. And even though it's a practice that you may have enjoyed in the past, this might very well be a practice you may not want to continue in the future, or you can expect questions like this in the future. And we can begin to establish a reputation that might have some gray area to it, and I don't think you want that."

At that time, we were bidding additional business with the city, and that factored into my conversation with them. I said, "We are potentially a finalist for some other projects. If you don't handle this appropriately, it will dog you through additional projects." When I presented to him the repercussions and the extenuating factors and the future business opportunities with the city, he reluctantly agreed to have that conversation with me. Then of course his first move was to pull in the lawyers.

As PR people, often our ethical questions get turfed to the lawyers and the legal team. That makes it difficult, because the lawyers want to say, "Well, this is legal. This is okay." And you have to say, "Hmm." Perception isn't often something that lawyers like to talk about because they may not agree with the perception.

Ethics and Conflict of Interest Advice

Jeff Hahn, Author, Breaking Bad News,[1] has further advice on resolving duty issues with legal:

> I always frame it with the best of intentions, and the intentions are oriented around two arenas. Public relations teams have to work the court of public opinion, while attorneys need to think hard about the courts of law. Court of law and court of public opinion are two very distinct and very rational arenas.
>
> If you can acknowledge those two swim lanes and ask questions that keep one another in those swim lanes, you have a lot better opportunity to solve the puzzle together.
>
> The challenge I hear most from PR practitioners is when general councils or outside attorneys jump the lanes, and they begin to try and make decisions for which they are not uniquely qualified. Gently steer people back into lanes through good questions, like, "Are you saying that as a court of law position or point of view, or from some other point of view?" Once you ask that question, you can nudge them carefully back into the swim lane. Typically, they're quite respectful once you recognize their legitimacy and the swim lane that they own, and they can understand the questions that you're asking are helping them see your legitimacy.

Mark Cautela, Head of Communications for Harvard Business School, also has insight into internal conflicts of interest—or when company and team before self is not ethically appropriate.

> In many places, you're taught three things, it's company first, team second, and you third. I agree with that for the most part, but the challenge is you're going to have to live with yourself. You're third, but you have spent the rest of your life with yourself. You might

---

[1] *Breaking Bad News.* 2020. Sky Harbor Farm Publishing.

leave that company one day, people on your team may come and go, but you have to live with yourself and the decisions you've made. People have told me always stay true to yourself, and I believe that because at the end of the day, you're going to have to live with these decisions a long time down the road.

Five Key Takeaways

How do we maintain the highest ethical standards in conflict of interest?

1. Disclose, disclose, disclose. When in doubt, disclose.
2. What you try to hide will come out eventually.
3. You do best by helping others before yourself.
4. Don't get too cute compartmentalizing to eliminate conflicts.
5. If your mother would be ashamed of you for the decision, don't do it.

CHAPTER 13

Enhancing the Profession

When I first started in public relations, my mentor Dave Close gave me some great advice:

Every interaction you have with the media or a client, your reputation either goes up or down. The agency's reputation goes up or down. The client's reputation goes up or down. Make sure what you are doing makes it go up.

The one thing he didn't say is that the industry as a whole has its reputation impacted as well. Ethical professionals always work to raise the reputation of the profession.

PRSA addresses this in its Code of Ethics when it discusses "Enhancing the Profession." The Code states:

"Public relations professionals work constantly to strengthen the public's trust in the profession."

The intent is to build respect and credibility with the public for the profession of public relations and to improve, adapt and expand professional practices.

The guidelines include: a member shall:

Acknowledge that there is an obligation to protect and enhance the profession.

Keep informed and educated about practices in the profession to ensure ethical conduct.

Actively pursue personal professional development.

Decline representation of clients or organizations that urge or require actions contrary to this Code.

> Accurately define what public relations activities can accomplish.
>
> Counsel subordinates in proper ethical decision-making.
>
> Require that subordinates adhere to the ethical requirements of the Code.
>
> Report practices that fail to comply with the Code, whether committed by PRSA members or not, to the appropriate authority.

I can sum it up even more simply by looking at it in a slightly different way, but it goes to an old Boy Scout maxim—leave the place better than when you found it.

Enhancing the Profession—DEI

One of the biggest areas where we are failing to enhance the profession is our failure with diversity, equity, and inclusion.

Neil Foote, CEO of Foote Communications and President of the National Black Public Relations Society, reminds people that celebrating success is not enough to drive diversity:

> Yes, we want to celebrate the wonderful successes of those diverse individuals who are getting opportunities. But we've got a lot of work to do. We can't sit back and think that everything is good. The operative phrase that I've been using is that DEI equals ROI.

Mike Paul, President of Reputation Doctor, pulls no punches in his frank insight into this issue when I asked him about companies woke-washing, DEI, and the need to quantify the efforts.

> It's bigger than that. It is not just putting numbers behind it; you have to actually hire people. We don't need another panel.
>
> Here's what I tell people, "I've been studying this for almost 30 years. I'm not a diversity, equality, and inclusion expert, I just happen to be black. I solve crises. This pops up, I look into it, I find the best practices approach to fixing it. This isn't rocket

science. When McKinsey and Deloitte[1] and others more than six years ago came up with studies that said, "When you start hiring people from intern to board member and every level in between to match the demographics of which you reside, operate, and serve, on average, you make one-third more money."

Think about how profound that is.

We've known this evidence for over six years. I sent it to every CEO you could think of and their boards. I said, "This is the playbook. Here it is. Here's a few corporations that have done it well, that have won a best approaches award. Utilize their example along with this data and this study."

If a CEO on average finds out once a year that something can make them one-third more money on average ... and you don't do it....

This is what I've said to CEOs of major corporations and their boards. "Guys, I got to flip it for you to wake you up. What that means is if you now don't do this, the only reason why you wouldn't is because you're either too prejudiced or too racist to do it. Why would you not want to make one-third more money? Why would that not be a good analyst question if you're a publicly traded corporation? Why would that not be a good journalist question? Why would that not be something that a shareholder raises their hand?"

Jessie Jackson buys stocks just to be able to do this and ask that question. Al Sharpton buys stock at his organization just to do that. The NAACP has learned how to do it. The National Urban League has learned how to do it.

Someone just a half hour ago said, "Mike, you keep talking about at least dozens of senior executives in each organization that need to be hired. Not sprinkles, not one or two. One or two's been going for two generations or more." I said, "That's true."

They ask, "Where do we find them?" I said, "It's an insult to even be asked that question, and you don't even know that. It's

[1] "The Diversity and Inclusion Revolution." January 2018. *Deloitte Review, Issue 22.*

an insult to also say that when you hear the three letters or the term diversity, equality, and inclusion and instantly respond to talk about interns."

I've been in meetings on panels, and I said, "Excuse me, nobody mentioned interns. How did we get to interns? Somebody mentioned three words, diversity equality and inclusion, why are you talking about a college scholarship. Why are you talking about an intern? Why are you talking about entry? Do you know how demeaning that is?"

There were several white women on the panel, so I said, "Let me break it down for you, this is the equivalent. You came in and wanted to talk about senior executive women and equity in pay and power and somebody just said, "Oh, I'm going to give a $1,000 scholarship to the Girls Scouts of Westchester County, New York." You're supposed to go, "What? What are you talking about? Who's talking about Girls Scouts?" It's demeaning. This is 2020. Wake up people, you can't do that."

We have people who have even married outside their race in senior executive positions, have children with someone else who is outside their race, children that don't look like them, and they still have conversations with me as though it's only a white world. I wake them up by saying, "You do realize your daughter's Asian, right?"

"Oh, Mike, where did that come from?"

Guess what? It's called the one-drop rule in America. You want me to shake you? Let me shake you. Let me wake you up so you don't sleep tonight. Your daughter's going to be called a chink soon. It's like, "Holy, why would you say that?" I said, "Because I'm trying to wake you up. No matter what wealth you give her, you can't stop her from having that experience. I can't stop my son who's as light-skinned as my wife from being called the N-word or being told his hair is different, and not in a kind way. I can go on and on. You need to educate yourself about these things. But it's not my job to constantly educate you."

You know what my job is? Let me give you this example of a CEO who is white, who stepped off of his board, and asked for them to replace him with an executive of color, in particular a Black male, which is the biggest area of crisis regarding DEI in any organization, at any level. It's the least opportunity and the least jobs filled. "Mike, my term's not up though, why would I want to do that?" "But you told me you wanted to help. You said, 'Wow, this DEI is something I'm getting to understand now. I want to do more. How can I help?' I'm asking you to help.

"You're coming up for your next board meeting, right?" "Yeah." "You should work in there and tell them you don't want to be in the board anymore." "But I like being in the board." Oh, I know you like being on the board. And I know of the 35 people on your board, 25 of them are white males. But you said you wanted to do something. The best way that you can help is to step down from the board officially and send a letter and have a conversation in that board meeting that says, "I want to help find my replacement, and I want it to be an executive of color." You see, because I know when 25 out of 35 on a board like this are white, certainly does not demonstrate the demographics of which we reside, operate, and serve."

When I use New York City as an example, people lose their mind. New York City is the capital of advertising, PR, finance, and insurance. In 2010, the demographics in New York City was 68 percent people of color. That was over 10 years ago. It's almost three quarters people of color now. They go, "Mike, oh my God, what does that mean?" "That means when you got 2 percent executives of color, you're at a you-should-be-sued level."

They respond "Well, Mike, you're not saying that we should have three quarters of our board and our senior executives of color?" "It's exactly what I'm saying. You're supposed to match the demographics. That is the best practices approach to businesses, you're supposed to match the demographics of which you serve and operate and are headquartered. It's exactly what I was saying, yes."

"Well, we're never had a discussion about that." I say, "I know. That's why you're in crisis. By the way, there is more of an educated population in New York City than most places in the world. There are some of the best universities. So, when you say you can't find them, they're here."

When someone was talking to me about a senior public affairs position within a global agency 10 years ago, and I said, "You do realize that the president of the United States is Black."

How many communication professionals are in that administration ... you're a headhunter, this is your job. When there are white guys in those positions in the White House, you make them vice chairman of your firm. You pay them a $500,000 salary plus bonuses and other structures to pick you. How many firms have hired Obama communication executives who had eight years or four years' experience?

I said that had to more than 200 hiring executives. You would think that they would have said, "Wow, what an amazing idea. I can go make money. Let me go after those people."

I said, "And here's what makes it even easier, they worked for the public sector. You don't have to buy a list; you can look it up. It's free. If they look Black, you might not be able to guess where they're from, but they're probably a person of color, right? This isn't rocket science." Nobody that I know who was told that did anything about it.

But the attitude is like, "You should have gotten to know me. I'm a CEO of a top five firm." I'm like, "What are you talking about? These guys are Harvard educated, Columbia educated, Yale educated, speak four or five languages, have the opportunity to start their own lobbying firms. You don't get it. You got to compete for them. But your mind can't fathom that because you have no experience in doing so. You see us as other; you see as less than. You see us as incomplete. And now worse, you now seek to interview us to check a box and don't give us jobs. We're not sitting around waiting for you."

Here's the irony, many of those people are making more money than the CEOs of these firms. If you tell those CEOs that, they think you're lying. They think you're making it up. They think you're exaggerating. Until these leaders can see us as equals or peers or something, they can't fathom, better…. Oh, God-forbid you say that word, better. We've done it in athletics. We've done it in entertainment. We've done it in many other sectors. We've become the president of the United States. Why on earth would you not think that some of us are better? Why could you not fathom that? Because your ego can't take it.

So, when I talk to friends who are saying, "Mike, what do you see coming? Biden's about to do some amazing things. He's already doing it in his administration." I said, "I warned you guys for years this was coming. It started with Obama. Now you're going to have a federal government with a vice president who's an attorney, who's going to be whispering in the president's ear every day, because every meeting is going to have dozens of people of color in it. White people are going to feel uncomfortable."

They're supposed to feel uncomfortable.

Troy Brown, President One50one, agrees with Mike Paul regarding the myth of no diverse candidates:

I talk to people and have these conversations, and they tell me, "Well, we just can't find qualified candidates."

Really? Have you heard of the tool called LinkedIn? Do you know about HBCUs? Do you know about UNCF? Have you heard of the 100 Black Men? Have you heard of NSBE for Black engineers?

There are just so many organizations with qualified people of color and not just for Black people. I'm talking about Hispanic organizations. I'm talking about Asian organizations.

If you want to really find them, there are a multitude, a plethora, a cadre of people out there for you to find. My grandfather used to say this: "Troy, people aren't stupid. They're lazy."

The people are out there, but business just don't want to find them. There are no excuses anymore. There is this thing called Google or Bing. If you want to find them, they're out there.

Ana Toro, APR, Fellow PRSA, CDC, also has insight into how we can advance the profession through diversity and inclusion:

> We have to go to the root of the problem and go to schools, high schools, and do PR for PR. If students don't know what PR is and how cool it is, they won't join. If school counselors don't know what this function is, how this profession benefits society and the many roles a PR practitioner can have, we won't have the number we want of diverse students entering to universities to study this career.
>
> With many Latino students, it's the expectation of your parents that you will be either an architect, doctor, lawyer, or engineer. If you tell them you are going to do PR, they're like, "What is that, and why?" There's a cultural aspect of it, but also, it's just the lack of knowledge of the many opportunities.

Mickey Nall, APR, Fellow PRSA, shares how he approached fairness and inclusion at Ogilvy Atlanta:

> I was running the Atlanta office, and as time went by, the staff became larger and larger. I had gotten out of the process of determining who could interview to hire. I had delegated that to a mid-level manager to work with HR. We were always very slow to hire because we wanted to be very careful to make sure we were matching skillsets with the need, and with the potential client.
>
> Suddenly I noticed, everyone I was interviewing looked just like this mid-level manager. Everyone was a Caucasian female, with blonde hair, size two. We were suddenly becoming the Stepford wives of PR agencies. I'm going, what the hell is going on here? I kept looking at it, well maybe this is what we're getting, I mean this mid-level manager is a phenomenal employee and revered by her clients. So, there was no issue with her performance.
>
> The next time internships came up, I called her in, and I said, I just feel like we are just sort of tiptoeing into diversity, and this is a huge problem in our industry. I don't understand with the University of Georgia, Georgia State, Kennesaw State, and Morehouse,

Spelman, and all of these colleges here in Atlanta, why everyone is female? That's all I said at that point, everyone's female, we need a more diverse group.

So, she said, "Oh, you want to hire more men." And I was like, well I want you to hire men and women who bring something to the table beyond our sameness. Our clients are certainly not that way.

This person was very upset with me and said, well let me just bring you the resumes, and you will see that I have chosen the most qualified individuals to come in for interviews.

Well, I flipped through about 25 resumes, and I found you could just tell from schools that people had come from and gender, that goodness it looked to me like, we had quite a few applicants that could be brought in.

I sat down with a supervisor, and just said, well here's what we're going to do, I'm not trying to get in your way, but I just have a duty to at least bring in qualified individuals and give them a shot, and see what happens. She was very upset with me.

But it became, as far as I'm concerned, the most ethical decision of my life to override someone I had handed off HR recruitment and interviewing, who did an excellent job with client work. And take it back and say, this isn't correct for me.

I literally looked through and found about 25 people that were great, I brought in 10, I hired a young man who went to a very small school, a small program. He worked with us for seven years, all the way to account director who then left to work for a major Georgia-based company and became a director at a global financial company. This young man would have never had the opportunity to experience our brand, to get that next job, to get that next job, because of someone screening inappropriately for the job.

I'm very proud to say over a three-year period, we became ethnically the most robust office in the United States for Ogilvy. We had more African Americans, Asian Americans, Hispanics, Latinos in our office percentage-wise, per capita, than any other office in the United States. It was something I was so proud of because we were walking the walk of the need to diversify the industry.

Now did we do a great job of inclusion? The industry is continuing to suffer from great diversity efforts, but less great inclusion efforts.

Diversity isn't just about hiring practices and mentoring. **Beth Monaghan,** Founder and CEO of Inkhouse, discusses steps every agency and business can take to help drive panel diversity:

The last time I checked, PR as an industry is only 8 percent diverse, which is pretty embarrassing when you live in a city like Boston, which is a majority minority city. Our staff should mirror the population in which we live if we ever hope to have the right kinds of ideas and be reflective of people who we work with. We are committed to that, and we've beat the 8 percent. We're at 11 percent which is still embarrassingly low and we're trying to go higher.

But one of the things that we're putting in place there to draw attention to it in the PR industry is our panel policy, which is basically that we will not sit on any panels that are all white or all male. So far, almost every time that I've told the panel hosts about the policy, they've diversified the panel.

There are some common mistakes when to enhancing the profession. **Cedric F. Brown**, APR, Independent Consultant, highlights why we can't just look forward:

The thing that was a little bit troubling about some of these organizations that put out statements about equity last year, is if you talked to their diverse employees, regardless of race, orientation, gender, what have you, many of them would say, "This organization doesn't treat me well. I don't feel included here."

Organizations need to be able to look within themselves before they put on an outside front. That's an ethical challenge. Many people don't like looking backward. They only want to look at the good things, but honestly, you can't know where you're going, if you don't know where you've been. It's going to take looking at and being able to atone for some of your past inaction toward racial diversity, gender diversity and orientation diversity. You need to be able to address some of those injustices that happened within your organization to be able to move forward and build trust, because otherwise, it rings hollow.

In a regular conversation, someone would tell a Black person who speaks about these injustices that, "Slavery ended in 1865. Get over it." That's discounting somebody's lived experience because racism is more than the ending of slavery. My take is just that slavery just evolved into different forms. And there are far more prejudicial practices that have been put in place that have prevented Black and brown and diverse publics' advancement in our society.

You need to be able to apologize for those past actions and just say, "Wow, I can't speak for my ancestors and our history. But I can commit to doing a better job and trusting your lived experience and listening to you as to how I can be a better support for you."

Enhancing the Profession Advice

Beyond DEI issues, **Perry Headrick,** Founder of Crackle PR, highlights why we need to fight sensationalism to enhance the profession:

Being honest with defensible claims builds long-term annuities. If you are coming out of the gate, gangbusters with all kinds of broad, indefensible claims, your revenues are going to be the victim, and your company's not going to do well. It's only when you harness the best of what you do and can show ironclad proof that your claims are accurate, that you can begin to have the platform to inspire people beyond the product or service that you're selling. It starts with having something that's real and then building on that with decisions that are beneficial for the company, employees, and stakeholders.

There's a certain degree of marketing and PR puffery that's okay. "One of the world's best, one of the leading." These kinds of things aren't necessarily terrible. But there are some claims that start getting a little bit ridiculous. There is the overall tone of some companies, you can see that they're punching way above their weight class, trying to kind of fake it until they make it. I understand the temptation. How many shots are you going to get in life to succeed with something? The temptation is there.

But discretion is the better part of valor. People ultimately learn that lesson at some point. Ultimately, everybody gets slapped back down to earth about what is real and what is true and what your True North ought to be.

Sabrina Ram, Founder and President of Blu Lotus, calls on the industry to stop putting profit over ethics:

We're seeing a lot of PR professionals putting profit over ethics and that's how we've gotten into where we are. As PR professionals, we have to understand that we hold a lot of power. We have the ability to shape the present and future for so many people, and there are short- and long-term consequences to our decisions.

Yes, we want to make a good living wage, and we want to be able to afford things that we want, but you have to ask yourself is that at the expense of a person or a community or an organization? Is that something that you can live with? Are you part of the problem, or are you part of the solution?

This is going to be an issue for a very long time. As a society, we are a very me society. What works best for me? What is going to help me get what I want? We need to start moving away from that from a professional standpoint and seeing the broader effects of what we do and how we do it.

Another ethical trap professionals fall into that does not enhance the profession is enabling toxic, abusive high-performers. **Lisa Gralnek,** Principal and Founder of LVG & Co., explains:

My toughest ethical challenge is something that we see a lot, which is when everyone knows that there's a bad player or a bad players, and they don't take action. When we're looking the other way, when there's this willful ignorance, or even straight up defense of bad behavior, I find that ethically challenging.

This came up in one of the companies I worked with. There was a real culture of this. Whenever there were big meetings where the entire organization would come together, senior female leaders would regularly coach and advise the younger female employees not to end up alone with a particular male executive.

There was one in particular who continued a meteoric climb through the organization. And yet, he had this very long track record of hitting on and harassing younger female employees. Everyone knew it but never did anything. It made for a pretty toxic work environment. That culture ultimately penalized everyone, people who don't speak up, and if they did, as I ultimately did, you were gravely limited in your career advancement. In my case, I was ultimately forced out.

Otherwise, your only choice is to put your head down and go along with it or to be one of these senior leaders who think that you're protecting your younger females by telling them about this. I just never understood that mentality.

This extends beyond discrimination or harassment. It's true whether a particular leader or manager takes credit for someone else's work, or when a firm or person in power overly exaggerates or spins the positive impact of their work. That poses such an ethical dilemma. The enablement of unethical behavior in defense of power is a challenge.

Changing this is a cultural question. This behavior of silence and complicity enables what I call the "Pass go, collect $200" behavior mentality that's so prevalent in large corporations and public institutions. You put your head down, you nod, you smile, you do what your manager tells you to do. You do the bare minimum to survive, and you're rewarded for it.

If you're going to say there's a no a-hole rule, or we don't tolerate harassment and discrimination or we're equal opportunity, you need to walk the walk. Let your values lead.

Values are the guideposts for driving forward. They are the GPS coordinates. In getting to a destination, you need to put those parameters in place, and you need to communicate them to the organization. I don't know if I'd say there should be a zero-tolerance rule, because everyone makes mistakes. But you certainly can't have everyone in the organization aware that there are exceptions and hope that you're going to be able to change the culture.

If you want to change the culture, it starts with your mission and your values. These values guide you from the mission to the vision to the destination and throughout the journey. Almost every large organization and many small ones have annual performance reviews or a performance management system. You need to tie values to these things.

You also need to enable people and encourage people to speak up. HR and senior managers have a very large role in this. You need to give them enough training and enough runway, so they know what to do if someone comes to them, and that they encourage it. You need to abide by values and not just shunt it under the rug, because it creates problems more broadly. If you're going to walk the talk, you need to make sure that the people who are the pathways and the conduits to that are taking action and trained appropriately.

Training

Training is essential for enhancing the profession. When training, first you need to understand what skills need to be trained. **Marlene Neill,** PhD, APR, Fellow PRSA, Assistant Professor at Baylor University, addresses this:

Ethical awareness is one of the skills that is lacking. There is a need for young professionals and professionals in general to be aware of the codes of ethics for their industry and be able to identify those issues, especially as we're all busy, and it can be very easy not to take time to think and deliberate about your decisions. Time constraint can be a challenge, in that we're so busy that you're not taking time to think things through.

Courage was listed as number one. Having that competence and willingness to speak up, especially to people who outrank you. That can be quite intimidating, especially early in your career, having that courage to raise a concern and ask the questions when something doesn't seem right.

Other types of skills were critical thinking and problem-solving skills. We can definitely see where that would be something you would need to develop early on in your career. Leadership comes over time. It was interesting that personal accountability came up on the list because you would think that people naturally would be accountable. But one of the concerns is that they have that personal integrity as well.

Other areas for training include the moral compass, having that personal values decision-making that's guiding your behavior. Strategic planning, research, and measurement, again, those core skills in public relations are also considered essential when it comes to ethics. One of the other skills that they listed in the longer list included business literacy.

What does that mean in the context of ethics? It can help you identify industry specific issues and understand the implications of the counseling that you're providing and how it can impact the business that you're working for. It gives you a better understanding about how to make your arguments and make a stronger case.

Blake Lewis, APR, Fellow PRSA, Principal and Founder of Three Box Strategic Communications, has advice for how to make ethics training a regular part of your culture:

We spend a fair amount of time discussing it. We have weekly staff meetings. We handle the agenda for the staff meeting in an interesting way. Anybody anywhere in the organization has the opportunity to create an agenda item saying, "Here's something I've seen that I want to talk about. Here's a situation that we as a team need to evaluate."

There are absolutely no filters. It doesn't matter if you are a junior associate or an intern, you can put something on there. The only expectation is that you can come to the table prepared to raise why is this relevant, why should we care? A lot of times ethical questions come up through just that observation of what's going on around us, whether it's the local community where we have an office, or anywhere in multiple countries where we do business.

When you set that sort of standard and you give that kind of freedom with responsibility, that's when you can start these conversations saying, "Hey, here's something that happened. How do we feel about this? What would we have done differently? Why would we have done it differently?" Inevitably, part of that conversation comes back around to what were the ethical considerations and how were they handled?

Matt Kucharski, APR, President of Padilla, also believes ethics training should not be an annual checkup:

We do ethics training, but it goes beyond ethics. It's training on our values. If you take those values, and you take that ethics training, you're probably 90 percent of the way there. We talk a lot about values to our employees and how to create a great work culture and create employee engagement, and believe me, that's incredibly important.

It's also a risk mitigation strategy. You make sure people are acting the way you want them to act. If they aren't, you have a reference point to be able to say, "You know what? That behavior does not follow these values and it's clear that these values are important to us."

You need to make sure that it's part of regular professional development curriculum and not, "Okay everybody. You need to go to our annual, once a year ethics training." That's a little bit like, "Take your vitamins."

Learning about the ethical dilemmas makes you a stronger practitioner because it allows you to see around corners. It allows you to be more strategic.

Other Advice to Enhance the Profession

One area where the profession hurts itself is with unethical measurement. **Melanie Ensign,** former Head of Security, Privacy, and Engineering Communications for Uber, emphasizes we need to stop confusing coverage with action:

> I focus more on, "What are the behavioral outcomes?" versus just the output.
>
> For example, there are tons of articles about how to secure your online accounts and how to use two-factor authentication. The Internet is just littered with these, whether it's a journalistic article or on a company blog somewhere, and yet we know within the security community we have abysmal single-digit adoption of two-factor authentication in most consumer communities. A lot of PR teams would consider those wins, because they got coverage, they created content. Yet, I have a hard time seeing that as a win, because it hasn't made a difference in securing people and getting them to use the tool.
>
> Part of that has to do with the limitations and the weaknesses of the tools themselves, and that is where I see the role of a communications professional being able to go back to their product team and say, "We've done X, Y, and Z on the comm side. If we're not moving the metric of people using these tools and finding them useful and valuable, we need to figure out how to fix the product." That's not a message problem. That message has saturated the market. That's where, again, being involved in those discussions in product development and business strategy early on can help influence, "Let's build something that protects people even if they never have to push a button."
>
> That's where Uber started. Our first two-factor authentication was on by default because we just knew that a lot of people weren't going to turn it on. So, the first iteration was to build something that would be triggered if we detected suspicious activity, and then chapter two of that was, "Let's give them an option of how they want to use that mechanism, whether it's a text message or security

app like Duo, But we started knowing that there was no amount of marketing PR or messaging that was going to convince everybody in the world to turn on this feature, so we built it on by default."

Some issues with enhancing the profession are industry-specific. **Peter Loge,** Director of the Project on Ethics in Political Communication, George Washington University, reminds us we have been facing the same challenges with political communication since the 1700s:

> Be honest, be clear, be direct, be skeptical but never cynical. It's a line I stole from a colleague who is a Republican Communications Operative and is now at a conservative site called The Dispatch. It's important to note America communication wasn't happiness, rainbows, puppies, and unicorns, and then along came Twitter, and the wheels came off. We've always been awful.
>
> In the Adams/Jefferson campaign, the supporters of Adams accused Jefferson of all sorts of things.... The President of Yale said that if Jefferson were elected president, our wives and daughters would be subject to legal prostitution. Jefferson didn't stoop to respond. Jefferson didn't get in the gutter. He hired someone to get in the gutter for him, and he paid somebody to spread stories in the partisan press that among other things, if elected president, Adams would invade France.
>
> Our political communication in this country has always been racist, lying, partisan, and awful. In 1946, George Orwell wrote that in our time, it is largely true that political writing is bad writing. He said that political rhetoric is a defense of the indefensible. It's rooted in pure wind. It's always been awful.
>
> Social media allows speed and scale in ways we haven't seen before, but it's a lot of the same. The response has to be the same. Don't be that person. Don't spread stuff you know isn't true. If it sounds outrageous, check it. Push out good messages. Just be better, and then hopefully policy makers and others can figure out ways to fact check stuff on the technological end. But the fact that I can't fix Twitter doesn't mean that I should be bad.
>
> I live in downtown Washington, DC. Sometimes there's litter in front of my house. I pick it up, and I throw it away. It's not my

job. Somebody else gets paid to pick up garbage. That one piece of garbage isn't going to change the world if I leave it there, but it's garbage in front of my house. I don't litter. One more soda on the street doesn't matter, but still, I shouldn't liter.

I view communication and social media the same way. Just because one more won't matter doesn't mean you ought to do one more. Just because one more bad thing online goes unchecked won't matter, you still ought to check it. Garbage is garbage.

Todd Van Hoosear, Chief Engagement Officer for Business Breakthrough Network, has a challenge to all of us to change the perception of PR:

The problem with PR is that we're really good at talking. We talk a good game. We don't spend enough time doing, and we're not appreciated for our ability to inform action. The best thing that PR can do as a profession is to insist on being in a position in which you're not an afterthought, that in which you are informing action and not justifying action. Words ring hollow, unless they're accompanied by action, and this has been made extremely clear over the past few months, as we've dealt, not only with COVID-19, but also with this crisis of consciousness that we're dealing with as a society in dealing with institutional or structural racism. Everybody's talking a good game, but what I love seeing is people taking that extra step and saying, "This is what I'm doing about it."

I'm donating money. I'm not just lecturing people in what is actual racism—although I've done a lot of that—but are we donating to causes? Are we walking the walk as much as we talk the talk?

The important part is not just walking the walk but being in a position where the CEO and management team sees you as a strategic resource for them and an important voice. PR stands for public relations. It doesn't stand for propaganda. Public relations is as much inbound as it is outbound. Representing the voice of the consumer, the voice of the public in the management decisions is a valuable and important thing to do.

I've been on many award committees. I'll never forget one conversation we had where it was down to two contestants. One of them was a small YMCA up in the North Shore that had suffered from a horrible incident with one of its coaches and had a terrible reputation problem. Because of that, PR had an opportunity not to make big splashy numbers and run a multimillion-dollar campaign, but fundamentally change how that organization operated from the ground up.

And the other campaign was the classic integrated marketing communications campaign that had great, incredible numbers in terms of engagement and visibility. The numbers were awesome. The sales impact was huge. We ended up going with the YMCA story because they insisted on having a seat at the management table, and they changed how that business operated. They didn't just change sales numbers. They changed how the business operated. They probably saved that organization.

Tami Nealy, Vice President of Communications and Talent Relations for Find Your Influence, highlights the role of mentors in enhancing the profession:

> Find a mentor early in your career. Find someone who you trust, who you can talk to about your personal growth and your struggles.
>
> "Here's what's happening. Here's what I've done. This hasn't worked. What could I do next?" I felt trapped in my own head. Being a young professional who wanted to be successful, I was afraid to speak up to other people and to be like, "well, you know, the company is run by men, and they have a lot more experience than you do at 32 or 33." But having those trusted mentors who believe in you, who see your potential, can be very, very beneficial.

Licensing is a topic that has been debated by the profession for decades as a way to enhance the profession. **Karen Garnik**, APR, President of Asociación de Relacionistas Profesionales de Puerto Rico, shares how Puerto Rico does it:

There are five countries in the world that regulate public relations. We have 1,500 practitioners with the required license on the island right now.

What you need to do is maintain continuing education. Just to give you an example, paralegals are not attorneys. You have an accountant, and then you have a CPA. It's the same thing. We have academic preparation. We do continued education. We adhere to a strict code of ethics. We have experience, and we provide the right type of advice, serious, transparent, ethical advice to all our clients, whether it be community relations or crisis management or issues management.

It is the whole spectrum of skills that we have, alongside the ethics and the integrity and the education, that separates us from the rest. There is no cost to have a required license. What you need to do is have the preparation. You need to have studies in public relations, and you need to provide the certificates that you do, the justification, and the evidence, and you need to continue developing professionally via education.

It's more an investment than a cost. If people want to work, they need to comply with the law. And this is a law. You need to comply with it.

Unlike the APR, you didn't have to study to take an exam or present to a board to begin. You need to maintain the skills that you have, improve them, and make sure that you work ethically.

Yes. There are sanctions, and you can be penalized. That's done not by the Puerto Rico Public Relations Association, but rather by the regulatory board. They're the ones who oversee those sanctions and any kind of penalizing effects it might have.

Jim Olson, former Global Corporate Communications lead for Starbucks and U.S. Airways, takes a broader look and believes we can help heal the fracturing of humanity by moving from impact to consequence:

To be frank, what we're facing right now is something much bigger than an ethics challenge. We're essentially looking at the fracturing of humanity and a crisis of humanity. The good news is that when we want to solve these mega challenges, we can do it. As we saw with COVID-19, we are capable of extraordinary acts of humanity as companies of all stripes from small startup companies to hundred-billion-dollar market cap companies like Google, orchestrated to do everything from converting their factories to manufacture masks and ventilators to airlines essentially giving up seats to fly doctors, nurses, and supplies across the country. We need that same orchestrated unity of purpose that companies use today to fight the global pandemic, to fight the equally big, if not bigger, virus of racism and injustice that has been plaguing our country for decades.

As companies and leaders, we need to move from looking at our leadership through a lens of being impactful to looking at our organizations and our leadership through the lens of being consequential. We need to move from trying to just be successful to actually being significant and having a ripple effect across our communities.

In 2015, at Starbucks, we rolled out an initiative called Race Together. When we developed that initiative, we asked ourselves, what could we do as an organization? How could we use our scale as a global organization, to create more empathy, more understanding, and more compassion in the wake of a number of racially charged tragedies that at that time had rippled across places like Ferguson, Missouri, and other parts of the country?

Race Together was not about pretending to have all of the answers or even any of the answers to racism and injustice in America. It was simply about starting the conversation, and conversation as we are seeing today is long overdue. We took a lot of heat for that initiative, and absolutely we did not get the execution or the sequencing perfect. But our intention to use our stores and our brand to have the conversations that so many people are saying we need to have now.... I have no regrets and would roll out that initiative again in a heartbeat.

When I think about being impactful, it may be from a customer perspective about driving extraordinary customer satisfaction. It may be about from a financial perspective, driving exponential double-digit bottom-line results. From a community standpoint, it may be about making a dent in a particular issue in the community.

Being consequential to me is ultimately about having the judgment and the leadership to weigh in on what ultimately are in many cases, life and death decisions. Boeing's a great example of a company that was faced with consequential leadership choices with the 737 MAX. Organizations today in the face of COVID-19 and the racial injustice travesties that we're seeing are going to need to make consequential decisions about how they operate going forward and how leaders lead going forward.

I can't let this chapter end, without repeating a plea I made as National Chair of PRSA in 2016. PR people need to stop saying "I hate math." The language of business is numbers. As PR pros, we can have a knock-down, knives-drawn fight over the Oxford comma. For 10 minutes, it'll be passionate on both sides. Executives feel that way when it comes to EBITDA and understanding how to read a balance sheet. The minute you say I got into PR because I hate math, you're cutting yourself, and you're cutting the whole profession, off at the knees.

Five Key Takeaways

How do we enhance the profession?

1. DEI is a moral imperative. Make it a priority. Prove it with actions, not just words.
2. Gen X and Boomers earned public relations a seat at the table. It is this generation's job to keep the seat and advance further.
3. Never stop learning.
4. If your actions are not enhancing the profession, your organization and your reputation—do not do it.
5. Don't say I hate math.

CHAPTER 14

Training Your Ethical Mind

Hopefully this book has provided insight into how other professionals identified and faced ethical challenges. The power of storytelling is the best way to prepare for the ethics challenges ahead.

People are more likely to make an ethical decision when they are given time to think. Yet, when it comes to marketing and communications, we are rarely given as much time as we need to think, plan, respond, and act, so we make snap judgments. It is when we make these snap judgments that people tend to make the most common ethical missteps.

The solution to this is to take a page from athletes and follow the 10,000-hour rule. We need to train our ethical mind. By regularly discussing ethical scenarios and issues with a mentor and their teams, professionals can better prepare themselves to make ethical decisions under pressure.

There are many models for making ethical decisions. From deontological, to the Six Questions checklist, to the Bowen model to the Wright/Martin model.[1] I have my own model. It isn't superior to the others, but it is a simple, replicable model that can be implemented and been tested over the past 20 years.

---

[1] D. Martin and D. Wright. 2015. *Public Relations Ethics: How to Practice Public Relations Without Losing Your Soul,* Business Expert Press.

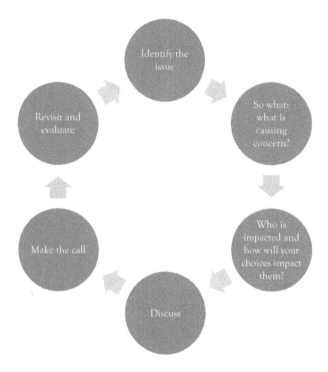

The McClennan Model of Training
Your Ethical Mind

- **Step 1: Identify the issue.**
- **Step 2: So what?**—Why is it bothering you? Is it a big deal? Discuss with others what is causing you concern.
- **Step 3: Who is impacted?**—Detail which stakeholders will your decision impact and how will it impact them.
- **Step 4: Discuss**—Never make the final decision without talking to at least one other person if possible. Seek other perspectives to uncover what you have missed or your biases. If they bring significant information to light, go back to Step 3.
- **Step 5: Make the call**—You can't debate forever. If you have the authority, make the call. If you do not have the authority—present your recommendations to the decision-maker and move it forward.

- **Step 6: Revisit your decision**—The sixth step, revisit your decision, is one that is overlooked in most ethical models. Most ethics models give you a framework for making a decision. But it is like Six Sigma. You can have a process and follow it perfectly every time. But if the process or the product is poor, all you are doing is making a poor product consistently. We need to evaluate and identity where we can learn and improve.

Part of improving is having regular discussions. Any model or plan doesn't work unless it is used frequently. Ethics training is like going to the gym. If you go once a year, it doesn't help. Make it at least a bi-weekly topic in every meeting. Ask people to identify ethics issues of the week. Share them with clients and your agency. Use the model to work through the issues. It is a great way to reinforce the importance you put on ethics and be ready for when you do face a significant incident.

Most importantly, if you are the team leader or the senior professional, do not share your opinion first. Let the dialogue flow and develop. When the senior person speaks first, it stifles discussion. Additionally, by being quiet, you may identify issues you overlooked.

Here's to great ethics discussions. Join me in raising your ethical voice and in enhancing the profession and the professional.

About the Author

Mark W. McClennan, APR, Fellow PRSA, is a strategic communication executive with 25+ years of experience with technology, fintech, consumer tech, and healthcare companies. He is the general manager in C+C in Boston, a purpose-driven firm, which was named Creative Agency of the Year by PRovoke Media in 2021. Teams he led have been recognized with more than 50 awards in public relations, including seven Silver Anvils. He was part of the team that received the 2021 Best of Silver Anvil Award for the COVID-19 campaign work with the Washington State Department of Health.

In 2016, he served as the National Chair of PRSA and drove the creation of PRSA's Ethics app. In 2018, he launched *EthicalVoices*, an award-winning weekly ethics podcast, and is a frequent keynote speaker and consultant on ethics and social media.

Index

OTHER TITLES IN THE PUBLIC RELATIONS COLLECTION

Donald Wright, Boston University and Don Stacks University of Miami, Editors

- *The Untold Power* by Melody Fisher
- *The PR Knowledge Book* by Sangeeta Waldron
- *An Overview of The Public Relations Function* by Shannon A. Bowen, Brad Rawlins, and Thomas R. Martin
- *Public Relations Ethics* by Marlene S. Neill and Amy Oliver Barnes
- *The New Era of the CCO* by Roger Bolton, Don W. Stacks, and Mizrachi Eliot
- *A Communication Guide for Investor Relations in an Age of Activism* by Marcia Distaso, David Michaelson, and John Gilfeather
- *Corporate Communication Crisis Leadership* by Ronald C. Arnett, Sarah M. Deluliis, and Matthew Corr
- *A Professional and Practitioner's Guide to Public Relations Research, Measurement, and Evaluation* by David Michaelson and Donald W. Stacks
- *Excellence in Internal Communication Management* by Rita Linjuan Men and Bowen Shannon

Concise and Applied Business Books

The Collection listed above is one of 30 business subject collections that Business Expert Press has grown to make BEP a premiere publisher of print and digital books. Our concise and applied books are for...

- Professionals and Practitioners
- Faculty who adopt our books for courses
- Librarians who know that BEP's Digital Libraries are a unique way to offer students ebooks to download, not restricted with any digital rights management
- Executive Training Course Leaders
- Business Seminar Organizers

Business Expert Press books are for anyone who needs to dig deeper on business ideas, goals, and solutions to everyday problems. Whether one print book, one ebook, or buying a digital library of 110 ebooks, we remain the affordable and smart way to be business smart. For more information, please visit www.businessexpertpress.com, or contact sales@businessexpertpress.com.

CPSIA information can be obtained
at www.ICGtesting.com
Printed in the USA
JSHW011950251122
33758JS00004B/44

9 781637 424186